❖ Dedication

W9-BPM-854

This book is dedicated to the memory of

Ruth Ross,
Helen Campbell,
and
Theresa Martin Franklin

So long, and thanks for all the support.

❖ Disclaimer

This book is designed to provide humor, education, and information on getting organized. It is sold with the understanding that the publisher and author are not engaged in rendering legal, accounting, psychiatric, psychic, or other mystical services. If such assistance is required, the services of a competent professional or witch doctor should be sought.

It is not the purpose of this book to reprint any information that is otherwise available to those in need of getting organized, or of any other organizers, real or imaginary. We'd like to think this book is completely different.

The organizing techniques in this book take a little time and thought to incorporate and use. Anyone who decides he or she is going to get organized overnight should think again. After all, how long did it take you to get as *disorganized* as you are? Rome wasn't organized in a day, you know. Be more patient with yourself than the people around you have been.

Every effort has been made to make this book as complete and accurate as possible unless we needed a nap 'long about that time. There may be mistakes, however, both typographical and geological in content. Therefore, this text should be used as a general guide and not as a "no-fail, one-size-fits-all" organizing system. There is no such thing.

How To Get Organized Without Resorting to Arson

A Step-by-Step Guide to Clearing Your Desk without Panic or the Use of Open Flame

Liz Franklin, C.A.
Cubicle Anthropologist

Clara Fyer™ Books
Alameda, California

Copyright © 2003 by Elizabeth M. Franklin.
Printed and bound in Canada.

All rights reserved. No part of this book may be reproduced in any
manner or transmitted by anyone, by any means whatsoever, electronic
or mechanical, including but not limited to photocopying, recording,
speeches, seminars, consulting, coaching, articles, excerpts, internet
posting, or by any information storage and retrieval system, except by
a reviewer who may quote brief passages. Everybody else needs
permission in advance in writing from the publisher.

How to Get Organized Without Resorting to Arson
ISBN 0-9719495-6-5

Published by
Clara Fyer™ Books
2532 Santa Clara Ave. #406
Alameda, CA 94501
Phone: 877-274-0844   Fax: 510-814-8003
http://www.franklinizer.com

Book Design by Liz Franklin
Illustrations by Liz Franklin
Edited by Chuck Franklin, Robert Whale and Leda Jean Ciraolo
Cover Design by Chuck Hathaway of
Mendocino Graphics/Cypress House
Layout Assistance: Foglia Publications

"They See Where Others Hear" by Keay Davidson
©*The San Francisco Chronicle,* reprinted with permission

Franklin, Liz, 1953-
    How to get organized without resorting to arson : a
step-by-step guide to clearing your desk without panic
or the use of open flame / Liz Franklin.
    p. cm.
    Includes index.
    LCCN 2002111112
    ISBN 0-9719495-6-5

    1. Paperwork (Office practice) — Management.
I. Title

HF5547.15.F73 2002   651.5
                          QB102-200607

QUANTITY DISCOUNTS are available. For more information,
please contact the publisher.

Furthermore, information in this book is current only up to the date of this printing — duh.

The author and Clara Fyer™ Books shall have neither liability nor responsibility to any person, entity, animal, goldfish, or disembodied spirit with respect to any loss or damage caused, or alleged to have been caused, directly or indirectly, by the information contained in this book or extrapolated from sleeping with this book under your pillow. In other words, if you read this book and still manage to lose things, you lost 'em, we didn't.

If you do not wish to be bound by the above, you may return this book to the publisher for a full refund, as long as your hands are clean and you have washed behind your ears.

❖Table of Contents

Chapter 1

The Secrets of Your Organizing Style

Chapter 2
How To Access Your Inner Organizer

Chapter 3
How to Find Your True Organizing Goal

Chapter 6
Nine Supplies You Need to
Get Organized

Chapter 7
Setting the Stage for
Getting Organized

Chapter 8
From Here to Efficiency

Chapter 9
Chaos Control: What to Do with All That Pending Paperwork

Chapter 10
How to Get the Help You Need
How much work is too much? Which items can you delegate? How can you store tasks until they are delegated? How can you get them to your helpers in the most effective manner? What helpers? 132

Chapter 11
How to Relieve the
Tyranny of To-Do Lists
How does your To-Do list work with all this? How can you turn your To-Dos into To-Dones faster and more efficiently? 147

Chapter 12
How to Simplify Projects

*Why does some paperwork take
so much longer than other paperwork?
Why does work keep expanding, or does
it just seem that way? What's the best
way to corral all the related items when
they won't fit into a regular file?*

Chapter 13
How to Maximize Findability

Chapter 14
How to Stay Organized Without Resorting to Discipline
OK! You understand your Organizing Style, Work Personality, and Access Type. You've verbed your papers, flowed your furniture, dated your priorities, and binned and shelved your projects. Now let's put it all together.

Chapter 15
How to Get Rid of Filing Fast
How will you ever get around to your filing, much less get to the bottom of it?

Chapter 16
How to Reduce Interruptions

Chapter 17
When You Get the Urge to Purge

Chapter 18
Recapping the Magic Questions

❖ Foreword

You're different. You don't work well with traditional methods, do you? No, you're unusual because you don't fit into any common system. In fact, you don't like to be told what to do at all, right? You're not a follower. You march to a different drummer. The usual rules don't apply.

It follows that no traditional organizing system will work for you. You've tried them all, haven't you? If you still haven't been able to get your paperwork under control, here's why: Traditional organizing books propose one system for everybody. You wouldn't think of buying one-size-fits-all pantyhose, golf clubs, or hats, so how could you possibly make use of traditional organizing methods that claim to work for everyone?

That's where this book comes in. Once you know *how* you are different, and *what* your special organizing style is, it all becomes clear. You start to see the methods to your madness. When you realize how to use those methods for *better* organization than before, you're ready to learn a different kind of organizing: one that not only gets your desktop cleaner, better, faster, but makes your whole life easier, more convenient, and even more profitable. Now you can have extra fun, extra time, and even extra money, where you used to have a big mess!

Now here's the extra-special good news: disorganization is not caused by weakness, lack of discipline, or personality flaws. It happens when, over a protracted period of time, there's no flow:

paperflow, traffic flow, and cash flow are all about flow. Think about it for a minute: isn't stagnation the theme of disorganization?

My objective in this book is to teach you organizing techniques that will keep your paperwork flowing smoothly, while showing you how to organize with your own special flair. Once you learn these techniques, you can use them to organize any part of your life, anywhere you live, for as long as you live, because they're derived from who you are.

I've been organizing people since 1979, and I *know* how important your work style is. I know what a big impact it has on your entire life. Traditional organizing recommends forcing the round peg of your special self into the square hole of somebody else's system. It doesn't work. Which is why you haven't been able to get organized. Which is why this book will work for you. I hope you find it refreshing.

Liz Franklin
San Francisco, October 2002

❖ Preface

Liz Franklin is definitely not crazy. There will come a point as you are reading this book when you say, "I wonder if this person is just totally a nutball," but she's not. I personally have been Franklinized, which is a little like getting a sensual massage and a little like being hit by a cement truck, but it worked.

There was method in her madness. I do not pretend to understand the method, but it works. My office finally makes sense. It has not become "clean," in the way that word is generally understood, but it has become functional. I have light where there should be light; I know where everything I need is; I have another new workspace created out of thin air and imagination and strange astrological incantations.

I am, in short, a satisfied customer. I believe that Liz Franklin can help you do whatever the hell it is you want to do. You must take some of her ideas on faith, but your faith will be rewarded. You will also have fun along the way, so much fun that you'll forget what you're doing is in fact one of the most tedious chores modern life has to offer.

So here's my suggestion: Curl up somewhere with a notebook, an adult beverage, and this fine publication. Read it with a great lightness of spirit. Write down any idea that occurs to you. Then take a nice nap. The next day, you will begin to change things in your office, and soon you will rule the world—or at least your neighborhood.

Jon Carroll, San Francisco

❖ Acknowledgements

I truly give thanks for the assistance and existence of Charles "Solve for X" Franklin, Margaret "Cat Lady" Azevedo, Precious "Take Us to The Light!" Stroud Chambers, Susan "Everything I Do Has a Reason" Jensen Kahn, Henry "Babelfish" Kahn, Kristin "You Go Girl!" Franklin, Cynthia Frank, Chuck Hathaway and the gang at Cypress House & Mendocino Graphics, Dorothy Foglia of Foglia Publications, and all my other Cross-Dominant friends and family.

❖ Introduction

The concept of "getting organized" has come to mean "let's make things all neat and pretty," but there's a lot more to organizing than mere neatness. If that's your main motivation for getting organized, you're reading the wrong book.

I've been organizing offices since 1979, and it didn't take me long to understand that, when my clients said they wanted to be organized, they really meant they wanted all their stuff to be accessible—just not all at once.

Your office can be neat and pretty, but still you may not be able to find things. In fact, sometimes the more things are put away, the longer they stay out of reach. We have been trained to focus on neatness at the expense of accessibility.

Check this out: If things are made accessible first, they can always be made neat later; but if the emphasis is on making them neat, they may never become accessible. It'll be too late.

Let's define accessible as convenient, which means convenient to *you*. Let's make accessibility the new name of the organizing game.

Accessibility means setting things up so you can find them easily; it means systems that conform to *you* instead of the other way around. It even means enjoying your work again.

This book is about *your* organizing needs. It's about how you access and how you like things arranged. It looks at how can you get organized in a way that's custom-tailored, that will work for you forever, and that gets you away from that mad cycle of inconvenience and blame.

Step into my world.

Chapter 1
The Secrets of Your Organizing Style

> *Learn about yourself, co-workers, partners, spouse, and others, and why each has a different Organizing Style. Why does each work so differently? How can you support them? What are the best organizing techniques to use?*

When I first began organizing offices, I'd make a recommendation to one of my clients and they'd love it. It would work and everything would be great. Then I'd give the same recommendation to another client and they'd hate it. It wouldn't work and everything would be awful.

Why? I had no idea, so I began experimenting. I eventually realized that different people accessed their stuff in different ways, and therefore needed different methods to get organized. Who knew? My mind boggled. Would I need four hundred organizing systems for four hundred clients? I began to search.

Then one day I was working with a totally delightful woman named Susan. She was jumping around frantically, trying to keep up with her own brain, which was spewing out new ideas, new projects, and new subjects before the previous ones had even gotten out of her mouth. We were two or three hours into laughing wildly, at which point I accused her of being a Sparklebrain. Her eyes lit up, she laughed until she nearly fell down, and she said over and over, "I'm a Sparklebrain! I'm a Sparklebrain!"

This led me to examine my other clients under a microscope (figuratively speaking, of course), and after some intensive research I found they could be divided into different **Organizing Styles**. Thus was born a new understanding.

Let's talk about the six Organizing Styles that I found, and which one is yours.

◁ The First Part of Your Organizing Style is Your Work Personality

There are two parts to your Organizing Style. The first part is your **Work Personality**.

There are three distinctly different Work Personalities: the **Sparklebrain**, the **Linear**, and the **Cross-Dominant**.

Your Work Personality reflects the way you plan, the way you think (or avoid thinking), and the way you organize mentally. In other words, the way you categorize things in your mind. It dictates how you put things down (literally, *where you put them*), and it results in a specific kind of physical organization (or disorganization—different shapes of messes!).

Which of these three Work Personalities fits you?

▷ The First Work Personality is the Sparklebrain

Sparklebrains are artistic, creative, idea people. They can be found zipping around, high on caffeine, starting projects left and right—but never quite finishing any of them. Following up is not their strong suit, to put it mildly. Bubbly, happy, and as enthusiastic as fireflies during mating season, Sparklebrains shower everyone with laughter, lightheartedness, and spilled drinks.

Sparklebrains make our world beautiful, interesting and exciting. They bring us gorgeous things: beautiful cars, cool-looking computer equipment, fine fashions, offices that look like operating rooms, and those cute little sweaters for dogs. Sparklebrains are trendsetters, motivational speakers, cheerleaders, procrastinators, and psychics.

Somewhere on another planet, Sparklebrains have fun taking only those jobs where they can start things. They just hire a couple of finishers and they're done for the day. (Hey! Idea! An employment agency that sends out starters for some projects and finishers for others! Oops—sorry—I sparkled!)

Here's how Sparklebrains plan: They envision a project, skip step one, start at step two, pause to visualize their goal (step twenty-three), go into a mild depression because they are not finished (before they even begin), forget where they are (because they are in too much of a big honking hurry), put off step three until tomorrow (which is about where they'd be anyway), abandon the rest of the steps, curse themselves out, and end up at step twenty-one. They drive everyone crazy, but somehow they create fabulous projects overall because they're *so* creative and because they're *so* great at enlisting others to finish their work for them. Whew! You can breathe now.

Do you know any Sparklebrains?

FAMOUS SPARKLEBRAINS THROUGH THE AGES

Famous Sparklebrains include Robin Williams, Goldie Hawn, Bette Midler, Shirley MacLaine, Tinkerbell, Richard Simmons, and probably just about everyone in Hollywood. On the TV show, "Friends," the Sparklebrains are Joey and Rachel.

◁ The Symbol for Sparklebrain is. . .

. . . ❋ because their thoughts shoot out in all directions! If you could open their brains and film the synapses, they'd look like a thousand Fourth-of-July sparklers! Wow, I get all sparkly just thinking about it!

◁ How to Spot a Sparklebrain

※ Sparklebrains start many projects but finish few.

※ Sparklebrains are highly creative, emotional, and social. Work can wait— until it's their turn to be in charge, and then *everyone* had better be working!

※ Sparklebrains are easily distracted. (Oh look! Post-its come in earth tones now!)

※ Sparklebrains change subjects quickly and often, and then forget what they were talking about. They're constantly asking you, "Where was I?"

※ Sparklebrains do well in the fields of entertainment, sports, party planning, modeling, hosting, as office receptionists, motivational speakers, TV talking heads, actors, socialites (does that pay?), fashion, and in all kinds of creative, glamorous, sparkly jobs. Almost everyone in Hollywood is a Sparklebrain.

※ When Sparklebrains are organized they have lots of original ideas, and they work especially well with people who are willing to follow them around and clean up after them. They have colorful offices, delight in serving on committees, and create welcoming work places. They like being part of a group; they get a lot done when there are people around.

☀ When Sparklebrains are disorganized they become upset. Nothing gets created, they are sick a lot, they lose papers, samples, and swatches, and they are late to meetings and events. They change the original plan completely, and the objective becomes unrecognizable. You can help by agreeing with them on the goal ahead of time, and then gently guiding them toward it.

▷ The Second Work Personality is the Linear

Linears are the opposite of Sparklebrains. Some people call them *pluggers* because they just keep plugging away.

We need Linears to keep us grounded, honest, and able to access the Internet. Linears are the finishers of the world. In fact, Linears spend lots of time finishing what Sparklebrains start. Linears like things simple and straightforward. Really, really, straightforward.

You know that U.S. Postal Service motto that states, "Neither wind, nor sleet, nor rain, nor dark of night can keep us from delivering your junk mail"? That's a good Linear motto. Nothing diverts them, even when you wish it would.

Here's how Linears plan: They set up the steps they are going to take, figuring them out ahead of time and in the correct order, and then they proceed toward their goal. They do not miss any steps. They keep moving in a straight line. If they make a plan, they stick to it.

On the other hand, if *you* make a plan, they ignore it unless it happens to match *their* plan.

When Linears are organized they work quietly, and they often prefer to work alone. If they run across a problem, it will divert them only until it's solved— then they get right back on track.

Most Linears can find anything in their offices. It might take a few minutes, but it's there and they'll find it eventually.

When Linears are disorganized it's because they have made too many plans, all of which take more time than they thought. They go into a kind of Alternate Universe where time doesn't matter to them, and they'll take as long as they need to finish each project. You cannot rush them, so don't even try. Weeks turn into months, even years, and the original project still isn't done and nobody knows why. But you do. Help our fellow Linears by re-prioritizing due dates on less urgent projects for them .

Do you know any Linears?

FAMOUS LINEARS
THROUGH THE AGES

Famous Linears include Mother Teresa, Ernest Hemingway, Jimmy Carter, Dilbert, Eeyore from Winnie the Pooh, the men who built the Golden Gate Bridge and Charlie Brown. On the TV show, "Friends," the Linears are Ross and Monica.

◁ The Symbol for Linear is. . .

. . . ✔ because they finish and check off each step before they move to the next. The check mark reflects their step-by-step, focused style.

◁ How to Spot a Linear

✔ Linears are intentional, dependable, logical, methodical, and reliable. They will rarely do what you ask unless they were headed down that path anyway, or unless they see the logic in it. Then they will get to it in their own sweet time. Not yours.

✔ If you try to change plans on a Linear, it won't work. They will stick to the original plan. They can't help themselves.

✔ Linears are always there for you. They are always there, period. Except when your network crashes; then they're at some computer convention and can't hear their cell phones ringing.

✔ Linears work well with any system or person that stays the same. They're even happy to wear the same shirt every day. You might find them wearing mismatched shoes, however, because they were too busy going over the Pythagorean Theorem one more time in their heads while they were getting ready, and because shoes are just not important in the grand scheme of things.

✔ Linears make good engineers, computer designers, programmers, architects, mechanics, mathematicians, researchers, electricians, teachers, plumbers, and scientists. Almost everyone in Silicon Valley is a Linear.

❖ **A Story about a Linear and a Sparklebrain "Getting It"**

I did some consulting with two guys in Hawaii — I'll call them Pete and Jim. They owned a small T-shirt company and were doing pretty well for just starting out: Their first year in business they grossed $250,000.

Pete was the gregarious, outdoorsy sales-type (Sparklebrain ✸) who brought in 99 percent of the income. Jim was the introverted, indoor, exacting type (Linear ✔), who made sure the paperwork—and everything else in the office— got done, and done right.

They called me because they needed help. They'd fought so often that their partnership was about to break up. When I got there and sat down with them, they weren't even speaking to each other.

To get them focused on the company instead of each other, I asked them to tell me everything that needed to be done every day. From opening the doors in the morning to turning out the lights at night, we listed every single task. By this time their lower lips weren't protruding quite so far, and they were glancing at each other carefully and even exchanging a few nods.

To finish the list, I asked them to tell me who was responsible for each of the tasks we had written down. We put Pete's name to the right of each task he did, and Jim's to the left of his. By the end of the day we had a pretty good start on two very useful job descriptions, and there were only a few tasks left unassigned. By this time they were actually talking to each other.

Because they focused on what needed to be done and divided up their tasks according to their Work Personalities, they finally realized they complemented each other. All they had left to do was to hire out the remaining tasks.

The following year, Pete and Jim grossed $650,000—almost three times as much as before. That's just one of the results people get from organizing by Work Personality!

▷ The Third Work Personality is the Cross-Dominant

The Cross-Dominant is a hybrid of the Linear and Sparklebrain Work Personalities. A Cross-Dominant might exhibit 80 percent Linear behavior and 20 percent Sparklebrain behavior, 60 percent Sparklebrain behavior and 40 percent Linear behavior, or any combination of the two. Cross-Dominants can use either side of their brain, and often use both sides at once. Their intelligence is tremendous, and when they focus on constructive tasks they can move mountains. Cross-Dominants have a "bigger vision" of what's going on, much like the view from an airplane.

Here's how Cross-Dominants plan: They look first at the main objective, then fit the rest in like puzzle pieces, filling this over here and matching that over there, figuring out what will work and what must be rejected. They are experts at triage.

11

Two Cross-Dominants can be as different as night and day. A Cross-Dominant who is 85 percent Linear and 15 percent Sparklebrain can see the entire scope of a project in advance, and can direct others to achieve resounding success. His Linear traits enable him to finish sixty important things before breakfast. He will probably die of exhaustion unless he becomes a very good delegator, which is a really, really good idea for all Cross-Dominants.

Another Cross-Dominant might be 50 percent Sparklebrain and 50 percent Linear. She's bubbly, outgoing, and wears those wild earrings—but, surprise! You can always count on her to do exactly as she says. Yes, she leaves early, but did you ever notice that she gets three times as much done as anyone else? That's why she gets raises and praise consistently.

When Cross-Dominants are organized they make great directors, managers, and leaders. Everyone follows them naturally, because their common-sense ability is so attractive and—well, so common-sense. They know how to view both the big picture and the small details at the same time, and they can make all the parts blend seamlessly. They also get a lot more done in a day than either a Sparklebrain or a Linear, in spite of the amount of time they spend helping other people achieve their goals (which is way, way too much time). They are natural nurturers, but they often forget to nurture themselves.

When Cross-Dominants are disorganized they feel as if they're at the tail end of a game of crack-the-whip. Their minds are rapidly switching back and forth from detail to overview, from their own needs to other people's needs, and from Project A to Project Z. With all of this going on they feel like they are hanging on for dear life. Be understanding, and try not to get in their faces.

Most Cross-Dominants didn't ask to be leaders, they just sort of ended up with the all of the responsibility and all of the power, and they are always mystified at how much there is still to be done. And most of them try to do everything themselves.

Do you know any Cross-Dominants?

FAMOUS CROSS-DOMINANTS THROUGH THE AGES

Famous Cross-Dominants include Leonardo DaVinci, Albert Einstein, Martha Stewart, Buckminster Fuller, Oprah Winfrey, Richard Feynmann, Bill Clinton, Oscar Wilde and George W. Bush. On the TV show, "Friends," the Cross-Dominants are Phoebe and Chandler.

◁ The Symbol for Cross-Dominant is. . .

. . . ✈ because Cross-Dominants have an overview as if from an airplane, and they're always zooming by at more than 500 miles an hour, unless they're just taking off, just landing, or at a complete stop. Just like a plane, they can't move at half speed without losing altitude and therefore perspective.

◁ How to Spot a Cross-Dominant

✈ You can spot Cross-Dominants by what appear at first to be mood swings, but if you look closer, they're just switching hats faster than Bartholomew Cubbins. They can see farther, figure out more sooner, and cover more ground faster than either a Linear or Sparklebrain. Imagine Martha Stewart directing people to meet a dozen deadlines at once, and you'll be on the right frequency.

✈ Cross-Dominants handle so many projects at the same time that they need a laptop to back up their laptop. They have so much information in their heads that it's easier for people to walk up and ask them a question than to do the research themselves, which is why people interrupt them with questions all day long, which is why they're so grouchy.

✈ Cross-Dominants are not exactly the most patient people on earth. You can recognize them by the way they roll their eyes, suck their teeth, hiss, and mutter, "Jeez!"

✈ Cross-Dominants know exactly how they want things done, but they end up trying to do everything themselves "so it'll get done right." If it turns out wrong they blame you, forgetting they took the project out of your hands a long time ago.

✈ Cross-Dominants think nothing of picking lint off the carpet while giving a presentation. Appearances mean little to them. I know one surgeon who uses a plastic dishwashing tub as a briefcase. (I mentioned this to a Cross-Dominant engineer who pointed proudly to his cardboard box.)

✈ Whatever needs to be done, Cross-Dominants do it as a matter of course. Go ahead; let them pick away. While they're working out that wedgie, they're probably also working on World Peace.

✈ Cross-Dominants can be found working as a pilots, astronauts, surgeons, entre-preneurs, inventors, philosophers, or in other "visionary" professions. Think "Renaissance person," and you've got the general idea.

✈ You can always count on Cross-Dominants to have reasons for everything they do. You can also count on them to forget to tell you their reasons—they think you've received them by osmosis. After all, that's how *they* figure things out, so what's taking *you* so long?

A SHORTCUT TO IDENTIFYING THE WORK PERSONALITIES

Since it's possible to run into a grumpy Sparklebrain ☀ or a delightfully outgoing Linear ✔, you can be fooled. To cut to the chase, first ask them if they are a starter (Sparklebrain ☀) or a finisher (Linear ✔). That should clear things up pretty quickly.

If they say, "Well, I start a lot of things but I don't finish much—only what I'm interested in," they're a Cross-Dominant ✈ for sure!

◁ **The Second Part of Your Organizing Style is Your Access Type**

The second part of your Organizing Style is your **Access Type**. There are three different Access Types: **Visual, Spatial,** and **Chronological**.

Your Access Type reflects the way you take things in: the way you look for and reach for things. It addresses how you seek lost items, and how you pick things up once you've put them down. It has to do with your habits, tendencies, and preferences—but most of all, it has to do with the way you *access*.

You'll need to set up your office according to how *you* are going to go looking for things, or you will never find anything. Have you ever asked someone for help organizing, and then been at a complete loss after they left? That was because their Access Type didn't match yours.

HOW DO YOU ACCESS THINGS?

1. 👁 Visual: Do you find things by *looking* for them?

2. ✋ Spatial: Do you find things by *reaching* for them?

3. 🕐 Chronological: Do you find things according to *when* you last used them?

Everyone accesses things all three ways (after all, we all have hands, eyeballs, and clocks), but you'll find you use one of these tendencies first and more often than the others. Read on and find your Access Type. If you're still not sure which it is, show your co-workers this list and ask them—they'll be able to tell you.

▷ Do You Access Visually?

People who access things by *looking* for them are called Visuals.

👁 Visuals have tall stacks of paper taking up most of their desktops. Not huge, messy mounds of mixed paper, just tall stacks. If you look closely, you'll see a system at work: Each stack represents a project. Visuals are ashamed of their stacks because they think stacks represent disorganization—but that's just not true. Stacks mean they access Visually, that's all. You know—"out of sight, out of mind." Visuals cannot find anything they cannot see.

👁 Take a look at what's behind those stacks: That's what your Visual friend *really* feels disorganized about. Is there a tall stack of paper in front of the computer monitor? It might mean, I don't know how to use this computer— and I hope nobody finds out! A stack of paper in front of the phone can mean, No more calls, please! A stack blocking the view of the person at the next desk might be telling a tale: It's possible they don't get along with that person.

👁 Visuals often wear glasses or contacts. The disorganized Visual may need to get his or her prescription checked—the problem could be solved as simply as that.

- 👁 Visuals respond well to colorful folders, large labels, bold markers, bright signs, and other highly visual organizing techniques. Any system that is too neat or too small won't work for Visuals, because if they can't see it, it doesn't exist.

- 👁 The other side of the same coin is that Visuals feel disorganized when they can't see their paperwork easily. For a Visual, "organized" means, quite literally, I see what I need to do.

- 👁 Any office that is Visually disorganized will have lots of stickies around the computer monitor, lots of decorations on the walls, and so many phone numbers and reminders pasted up at eye level that no one could concentrate.

▷ Do You Access Spatially?

People who access by *reaching* for things, often without even looking, are called Spatials.

- 🖐 Spatials like the paper on their desks to be at right angles or fanned out like a deck of cards.

🖐 Spatials often touch people lightly on the wrist, arm, or back while talking to them, and they often move around to help their thinking process.

🖐 When Spatials finish a task, they crumple the To-Do Note and toss it away. This is their physical way of saying, "All done!" (as opposed to Visuals, who simply turn their eyes toward the next project).

🖐 Spatials who lose things can find them by physically retracing their steps, or they can jog their memories by walking around and waving their arms. To help them, ask, *Where* were you using it last?

🖐 Spatials must have their desktops clear. They cannot even *begin* to work unless they can move their arms, swing their feet, and reach freely for whatever they need. Their immediate surroundings are of utmost importance to them. For Spatials, "organized" means, I can put my hands on things easily.

🖐 An office that is Spatially disorganized will have boxes under the desk, furniture that blocks traffic, clutter on all surfaces, files too far away to reach, and a badly positioned chair pad (which means they are continually rolling off the edge, jarring their peace of mind).

▷ Do You Access Chronologically?

People who access *numerically*—by time, date, and "the bottom line"—are called Chronologicals, or Chrons.

🕐 You can recognize Chrons by their love of clocks, numbers, and electronic devices. They're the type that's always saying, "I'm right on time, what are *you* waiting for?" Or else they're always a day late and a buck short. Either way, it's all about numbers. Before they can talk to you in comfort, they need to arrange their calendar or Palm Pilot in front of them—that's "access" to a Chron.

🕐 If Spatials want to know where they're supposed to be, Chrons want to know how long before they have to be there.

🕐 Chrons can work from their cars, kitchen tables, multiple offices, or even public transit, as long as no one changes the order of their papers. They arranged their things according to *when* they happened, and they expect to come back and find nothing changed.

🕐 Watching a Chron search for something is like going along on an archaeological dig. A Chron can look at a stack of stuff and pull what he needs instantly, knowing the oldest is on the bottom and the most recent on top.

⏱ Chrons are the only Access Type that can work with pending systems effectively, because they are so time oriented. They like numbered folders, wear beepers with numeric codes, and have electronic devices on each hip. Talk to these people in numbers—it will save a lot of time.

⏱ Chrons access things by *when* they last used them: "Let's see, it was right after last week's meeting..." And darned if they don't find them that way, too! For Chrons, "organized" means, I can find it when I need it.

⏱ An office that is Chronologically disorganized has no clock, calendar, or calculator within easy reach. The disorganized Chron doesn't know what time or day it is, which *really* ticks her off. Their paperwork may look neatly stacked, but the dates have gotten out of order. Disorganized Chrons can never find anything *when* they need it.

HOW THE DIFFERENT ACCESS TYPES GO ABOUT FINDING THINGS THEY'VE LOST

Let's say you've lost something, and you want your friend to help you find it. Here's how you can tell which Access Type he is: Listen to what he asks you.

The Visual 👁 will ask you where you *saw* it last.

The Spatial 🖐 will ask you *where* you were when you used it last.

The Chron 🕐 will ask you *when* you had it.

Coming up, we'll talk about how each of these types *must* organize in their own special way, and why they will *forever* feel disorganized if they try to follow someone else's rules.

A RECAP OF YOUR ORGANIZING STYLES

The summary below will remind you of the symbols for your Organizing Style. Remember, you have one from each category:

A. Your Work Personality:
You are either a
- Sparklebrain ☀
- Linear ✔ or
- Cross-Dominant ✈

B. Your Access Type:
You are either a
- Visual 👁
- Spatial ✋ or
- Chronological 🕐

Which symbols should you watch for?

Use this handy guide to remind you of the symbols for your Work Personality and Access Type.

Your Organizing Style:	Your Access Type:	Visual	Spatial	Chronological
Your Work Personality:		👁	✋	🕐
Sparklebrain	☀	☀ 👁	☀ ✋	☀ 🕐
Linear	✔	✔ 👁	✔ ✋	✔ 🕐
Cross-Dominant	✈	✈ 👁	✈ ✋	✈ 🕐

Chapter 2
How To Access Your Inner Organizer

> *What's an Inner Organizer? Do you have one? If so, how can you use it to make your organizing project easier?*

Here's another thing you should know about yourself: whether you have an **Inner Organizer** you can call upon in times of chaos.

Most of the people I work with have the ability to access their Inner Organizer, which gives them a terrific benefit.

This Inner Organizer is called **synesthesia**, and the people who use it are called synesthetes, or are said to be synesthetic. Numbers vary depending on who's reporting, but generally it is said that only 1 in 200 people are synesthetes. Other reports state that everybody is synesthetic but most people do not realize it.

Synesthesia is best described as *linked sensations*: Synesthetes can *hear* colors, *see* smells, and make amazing, unusual connections that other people have never experienced. These sensations apparently remain consistent to the individual throughout their lives.

Does this seem like it would make organizing harder? It actually makes it easier, because synesthetes sense— and can set up—dependable links that make their stuff easier to find. Here's some more about synesthesia.

26

The following is an article about synesthesia
by Keay Davidson, Science Writer
© *The San Francisco Chronicle*
Reprinted with permission.

They See Where Others Hear
To a synesthete, making sense is in [the]
eye, ear, nose of [the] beholder

The letter "c" is light blue, "a" evokes a
sense of "weathered wood," and "r" feels like
"a sooty rag being ripped."

So wrote the novelist Vladimir Nabokov
—and he wasn't simply being poetic. He
was one of a tiny band of humans gifted
with synesthesia, an unusual neurological
ability to mix sensory signals from different
organs.

Do you literally see all vowels bathed in
a yellowish or greenish glow? Or hear a
musical note when you see a certain color?
Or smell a particular odor when you feel a
certain shape, such as the roundness of a
ball? Maybe you were too embarrassed to
admit sensing such unorthodox sensations;
maybe friends or family dismissed you as
"strange" or "in need of counseling."

Well, you're not alone, scientists say. As
many as one in a few hundred humans may
be synesthetes. And they're coming out of

the closet and getting organized: The first national meeting of the American Synesthesia Association will be held at Princeton University on May 19 (2001).

They're also declaring fierce pride in their unusual sensory traits: "Synesthetics say they wouldn't give it up for the world. They think their life is enriched by it," says Lynn C. Robertson, a leading authority of synesthesia and other unusual neurological conditions at the University of California at Berkeley's psychology department.

Research on synesthesia is shedding light on brain mechanisms in general, Robertson writes in today's issue of the journal Nature.

For example, she says, research from Australia—reported in the same issue—is helping to clarify the old scientific debate over whether one must be consciously aware of certain sensory information in order for the brain to assemble it into the coherent impressions we have of reality: say, of a rolling red ball or a passing white dove.

Compared to the relatively drab worlds of nonsynesthetics, some synesthetics seem to inhabit a "Yellow Submarine"-type realm where colors sing, shapes exude sensual smells, and numbers and letters illuminate their field of view.

Private Party

Yet synesthetics enjoy these Technicolor, symphony-in-their-head perceptions in private. Typically, no one around them is aware of their sensual unorthodoxy, save when the synesthete makes a revealing remark: something like, "Oh, what an azure 'v'!" or "That chicken doesn't have enough points on it."

Bay Area synesthetes are being tested at UC Berkeley by Robertson's graduate student, Noam Sagiv.

Sagiv, a doctoral candidate in psychology, said yesterday he has used the internet to track down a few dozen synesthetes from the Bay Area, and plans to test several more in the coming weeks. He plans to report his initial findings at the Princeton conference in May.

In no way is synesthesia a "disability," Sagiv and other experts stress.

A Colorful World

"The vast majority of synesthetics we talk to actually enjoy their synesthesia," he said. "They wouldn't want to live in a world that is less colorful.

"And synesthesia doesn't only involve just colors. It can also involve auditory, olfactory (and other) senses.

"The only synesthetes who ever complain about synesthesia," Sagiv adds, "are those who hear (annoying) sounds when they see things like bright colors. However, this is very, very, very rare."

One Australian synesthetic complains of hearing a high-pitched, headache-inducing sound when he sees a dark red curtain, says Anina Rich, a graduate student at the University of Melbourne. She led the Australian team, whose synesthesia research appears in today's Nature.

For Rich, perhaps the most rewarding aspect of her research is when "I get phone calls from people who say, 'Wow, I've just heard about (your research) on the radio, and I finally realized there are other people who see colors or taste shapes, too.' "

◁ How Does a Three Smell? Take This Test!

Find out if you are a synesthete by taking the test below. It has no right or wrong answers, and your answers may even seem odd—don't worry, the questions are odd! Just say the first answer that comes to mind and move on.

For best results, take this test with a friend or co-worker. Have her read the questions to you out loud. Make sure she writes down your answers.

Now, take the test again. This time, keep your eyes closed when you answer (this is important!). Report on what you *see* in your mind's eye, not what you think you *should* say. Have your friend make another column called, "Eyes closed" and write down your new answers there.

If no answers comes to mind readily, move on. Trying too hard will result in useless answers.

When you're done, open your eyes and compare the two lists. Do they differ? If so, whenever you answer a question in this book, answer it with your eyes closed. That's the best way to set up your new organizing system. Your Inner Organizer won't have it any other way.

THE SYNESTHESIA TEST

1. How does a three smell?

2. What color is your favorite song?

3. How does a year sound?

4. What number is Thursday?

5. What flavor is June?

6. What color will keep you from doing tasks?

7. Name somebody you work with: What color reminds you of that person?

▷ There Are No Wrong Answers

If you had answers—any answers—for two or more of these questions, you are a synesthete. In fact, the wilder your answers were, the more you can consider yourself a member of this most unusual club.

If you could answer only one question, if you had a blank look on your face, or if you had to struggle and try to make up answers, you are *not* a synesthete. No matter. This will be one less thing for you to think about.

If you *are* a synesthete and don't use it in your organizing system, you *will* run into problems. Since you are already accustomed to layered ideas, unusual colors, and unique connections, applying traditional organizing rules on top of all that will cause you to get mixed up and lose your way.

Stick with what your Inner Organizer tells you, don't believe the traditional organizing rules you hear, and you'll do just fine.

▷ Why You Can't Get Organized in Traditional Ways

Ask one synesthete about a song, and he will tell you what he was doing the first time he heard it. Ask a second about her family, and she will tell you what flower each one "is" to her. Ask a third about fruit, and he will make up a song on the spot. If you aren't synesthetic, none of this is making any sense to you, so just skip ahead to the next chapter.

If it *is* making sense, you are starting to realize that no ordinary organizing system will work for you, because it leaves out a huge part of who you are. The depth, flavor, and color you need just won't be there.

This explains why, when some corporations demand that everyone use the same organizing or time management system, some people can't make it work or don't even try. It's just too rigid, flat, or even one-dimensional for them, and they know it before they begin.

HERE'S HOW THE DICTIONARY DEFINES SYNESTHESIA

Synesthesia:
(Syn-ess-THEE-zha)

1. A condition in which one type of stimulation evokes the sensation of another, as when the hearing of a sound produces the visualization of a color.

2. The description of one kind of sense impression by using words that normally describe another.

Synesthete:
(Syn-ess-THEET)

A person who experiences synesthesia, as by having a secondary sensation of sound as color, or of color as sound.

American Heritage Dictionary,
Third Edition, Houghton Mifflin © 1992

For more on synesthesia, go to
http://www.users.muohio.edu/daysa/synesthesia.html

Throughout this book, I've made it easier for you synesthetes to access your Inner Organizer by marking pertinent passages with this symbol of an ear 𝒟 . If these passages don't "ring true" for you (a particularly synesthetic phrase: why does the truth "ring?"), just ignore anything with the ear symbol next to it.

So what does synesthesia have to do with getting organized? Let's find out.

◁ What's That on Your Mind?

Synesthetes 𝒟 who try to get organized in the traditional way just can't. If they don't know they are synesthetic they may beat themselves up for not being "disciplined enough."

Synesthetes without custom-tailored organizing systems are forced to ignore the many interesting layers and rich possibilities they could have if only they knew what was missing.

For example, a synesthete may "know" that urgent files are "supposed to be" blue. But if she denies her Inner Organizer and makes her urgent files red (because that's what all the traditional organizing books tell her to do), she'll never find them, because she'll still be looking for the blue ones she saw in her mind's eye.

I have synesthetic 𝔇 clients who can't see a folder right in front of them when it doesn't look as they imagined it would. A more reliable way to set up a system for a synesthete is to have her close her eyes and tell you how she envisions things, then follow it exactly.

If you are synesthetic 𝔇 and use it to your advantage, you'll end up with an unusual and highly effective system that will work far better for you than any traditional system. Just remember, it won't work for anyone else.

If they tried it, they'd find it didn't have enough points.

Chapter 3
How to Find Your True Organizing Goal

> *When people talk about getting organized, they can mean very different things. What do you mean when you say you'd like to be organized? What is your true organizing goal?*

◁ What Organizing Is and Isn't

Because everyone expects getting organized to do different things for them, let's go over what organizing is and what it isn't.

▷ What It Is

Getting organized means

- Making sure everything you need is easily accessible

- Keeping it simple so you find things often and seldom lose anything

- Leaving time to eat, sleep, and see your family

36

- Using a system that works well so it *stays* organized without baby-sitting, cross-referencing, or constant updates

- Enjoying a system that matches your Organizing Style

▷ **What It Isn't**

Getting organized does *not* mean

- Rewriting lists, logging time spent doing each task, or coding by priority (A, B, C labels)

- Analysis, therapy, or deciding that *you* are the problem

- Buying forms or notebook pages that are so special you can't work if you run out of them

- Trying time management (no one can manage time; they can only adjust their work methods)

- Buying more and more electronic equipment that doesn't make your life any easier

- Trying to get organized with a generic (one-size-fits-all) system that doesn't fit *you*

✓ What's *Your* Organizing Goal?

Take this time to think about what you want to achieve, really. Not what your spouse, partner, or roommate has been nagging you to do. For the time being, let's consider that irrelevant.

Organizing is a relatively new profession, and organizers can help you in many different ways. Whether you hire help, work with a friend, or get organized by yourself, this list will help you find out exactly what you want. After all, you don't want to discover you've hired a full time-bookkeeper when you really needed a cleaning person—or vice versa.

Some people say they are organized when their filing is finally done; others when they are financially solvent. Still others feel organized only when all the papers are cleared off their desks. Read the twelve kinds of organizing described below and decide which one— or ones —will work for you.

TWELVE KINDS OF ORGANIZATION: WHICH ONE DO YOU NEED?

1. Bookkeeping: the reporting of numbers after the fact (the money is already spent, the income is already earned). To a

bookkeeper, "get organized" may mean, "get the checkbook balanced," or "input records to a computer program."

2. Cleaning: to a cleaning person, "get organized" means, "dust, wipe, wash, and put things away."

3. Clerical: clerical work includes filing, record-keeping, answering phones, and may include reception. To a clerical person, "get organized" means, "keep things neat and record transactions accurately."

4. Coaching/Consulting: the analysis of and recommendations for improving your current work methods. To a coach or consultant, "get organized" means, "analyze and recommend," not necessarily "make changes."

5. Counseling: a qualified professional (such as a therapist) can help you get your sanity back. Such a person advises and guides you with words, concepts and emotions. To a counselor, "get organized"

means, "learn to sort out your feelings and emotions."

6. Delegating: passing work to someone who can do it as well as you, or better. Some people think "getting organized" means, "getting more help." If this is you, plan carefully—getting a friend to help could result in their Organizing Style overriding yours. Whomever you hire, give them clear instructions about job descriptions, expectations, who will supervise, and how each person fits into the overall organizing effort.

7. Filing: the placement of papers into files, which could include making new files or setting up new filing systems, but does not include decision making in any other part of your office. To a filing person, "get organized" means, "bring the filing up to date."

8. Financial Planning: the management of your money with the goal of increasing your net worth. Financial planners advise you on how to improve

your financial well-being. To a financial planner, "get organized" can mean anything from "diversify your portfolio" to "file your taxes on time for a change."

9. Ordering: to put things with others like them alphabetically, by date, in numerical order, by size, by color, or by any other category. To the orderly person, "get organized" means, "put all like things together." This option may not result in your stuff actually being accessible to you.

10. Space Planning: from interior design to moving furniture to building, space planners think of "getting organized" as meaning, "maximize the use of the space."

11. System Change: an overhaul of your entire work system to improve access, efficiency, paper flow, space, finances, furniture, delegation/ supervision, storage, concentration and traffic. System Change people need to be Cross-Dominant, and are either Chron or Spatial.

12. Traditional Organizing: may include bookkeeping, filing, sorting, cleaning, putting things away, or just advice on how to do such work yourself. To traditional organizers, "get organized" means, "standardize everything." Traditional organizers are not necessarily trained to solve disorganization for individuals.

What's *your* organizing goal?

Chapter 4
You're Not Disorganized, Your Office Is!

How does paper flow through your office? If it's not flowing, why not? Read this chapter and the next one before you start blocking out time to get organized.

Most people who call me for help say they don't know how things got so bad. They often feel guilty or embarrassed because they have read traditional organizing books that equate disorganization with personal weakness. Hogwash! I don't believe in emotional causes of disorganization, except in extreme cases (and even then, I think there may be extenuating circumstances).

Time and again, my experience has proven that most disorganization is caused by yucky flow: Paper flow, traffic flow, even cash flow—they're all related.

This chapter deals with the beginnings of flow. Together we're going to set up your office so your paper flows more smoothly and naturally into your office, to your desk, through your paper flow process, and back out again.

◁ Where Paper Flow Starts

Paper flow starts at hand level. It comes into your office via people's hands. You open the mail with your hands, you take it from the fax, printer, or copier with your hands, you scribble notes with your hands, clip interesting things out of the paper with your hands, and input to your computer with your hands.

Why all the emphasis on hands? So you'll remember this important secret of organizing: paper always lands on the *first available hand-height* surface. And what do we find at hand height? Furniture. Paper lands, and stops, wherever there is a convenient piece of furniture. Preferably a flat piece of furniture, but almost any hand-height furniture will do.

▷ Catchers and Blockers

I call flat surfaces *catchers*, because when paper lands there, it stays there.

Catchers include tempting places to leave paper like:

- the top of a file cabinet

- the floor

- a chair

- across the T where two cubicles join at the top

When people carry paper into your office, the farther they have to walk to get to your desk, the more likely they are to set it down along the way. If your office is set up like a maze, there will be paper on every flat surface—every catcher—between the door and your desk.

The opposite of a catcher is a *blocker*. Blockers are tall furniture, walls, or other vertical surfaces where paper can't possibly land. Papers will stack up *beside* blockers, or *next* to them, but never on them.

Look at your office and find the tall furniture. Are there papers in front of it or beside it? If so, you can be sure it's a blocker.

Blockers include:

- doors

- folding screens

- tall file cabinets

- tall plants or trees

- closets (if the doors are closed)

▷ The Secrets of Flow

Now that you know where paper lands and why, and how it's caught or blocked, you've been initiated to the secret of flow. Flow turns out to be one of the most important tools to use in getting organized.

When you've read the upcoming chapter and smoothed out the flow, you'll notice a big change: You'll see papers and projects start to *move* instead of just shuffling aimlessly back and forth across your desk or stagnating on the floor and the furniture.

When you're organized, you'll enjoy an increased energy level, an improved career path, maybe even increased income. Remember, keep chanting, "Traffic flow, paper flow, cash flow." Organized flow can mean the difference between progress and despair.

When you understand how to *flow* paper, people and objects smoothly around a room, your whole perspective shifts and just about everything becomes much easier. Take heart! As you'll see in the next chapter, it's a lot easier than you think.

Chapter 5
How to Blame Your Disorganization on Your Furniture

Why does disorganization have so much to do with furniture placement? Could getting organized be as simple as moving the furniture?

Be sure you read this before you go out to buy the organizing supplies described in chapter 6.

The placement of your furniture is an extremely important organizing tool. If you're disorganized it may not be your fault—your furniture could be the culprit!

We're not talking *feng shui* here. There's a feng shui organizing book that says mess causes stress. That seems backwards to me: I believe stress causes the mess. For example, it's stressful to walk back and forth around and around a lot of furniture all day long. It's stressful to twist your back, strain your arms, and bend to reach things. It's much easier to drop things halfway and give up on the filing. And don't you think it's stressful when you can't find what you need? It breaks your concentration and stops your work cold, doesn't it?

So we can blame the mess on the stress, and we can blame the stress on the furniture arrangement. But we can't blame any of it on you; you had no way of knowing furniture could hold such secrets.

Try this on for size (a very Spatial phrase!): If it's inconvenient for you to put things away, you won't do it as often. Doesn't that make sense? And when you finally do put things away, you'll resent it because in some secret part of your brain, your Inner Organizer, is hollering, "This shouldn't be so difficult or take so long!"

It follows, then, that the more convenient it is for you to move around your office, the more organized you will be. Convenience is another very important organizing tool.

If you don't believe me, try this: Move your desk even farther from your office door, then put a table halfway between. Paper will begin to stack up on the new table, stopping far short of your desk. You've just created a catcher. Leave it that way and notice the paper never gets to your desk. Remove it and move your desk back, and presto! You have repaired the flow.

If your paperwork is not flowing as you want it to, one of the easiest fixes is to simply rearrange the furniture. Embarrassingly low-tech, yet extraordinarily effective.

We'll talk more about furniture placement in just a minute, but first let's take a look at a typically disorganized office flow.

HOW A TYPICALLY DISORGANIZED OFFICE FLOW WAS SOLVED

Early in my career, I organized a group of graphic designers who called me because they had become disorganized without knowing why.

In this office, four people worked in a long, narrow room where there was only one possible configuration: four desks in a row, side by side. The first thing I did was ask how each person's duties related to everyone else's (called *proximities.*) Their answers showed me how the paper moved.

The person at desk 3 opened the mail. Then she gave the invoices to the person at desk 1 who approved bills to be paid. They then went to the person at desk 2 who paid the bills, to desk 4 for a signature, and back to desk 3 to be mailed.

You can figure out what was happening when you look at the diagram: complete confusion!

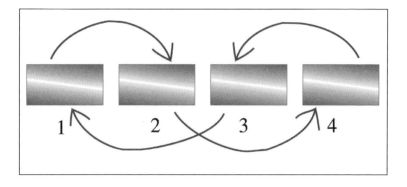

Those invoices were just one set of papers. Multiply this by hundreds of sets and you begin to see the problem.

I suggested they rearrange their furniture to match the *actual* flow—the way their paper-work would progress if it could move natu-rally. We set up the desks to support paper flowing from the mail-opening station at the desk nearest the door, then to the second desk for the second part of the process, the third desk for the third part, and so on.

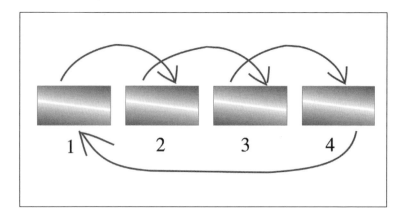

Their jaws dropped, they stared at me, at each other, at me again, then said, "Let's do it!"

Their entire office was organized in two hours without any papers being moved at all.

◁ Good and Bad Arrangements

Most furniture, cabinet, and space designers know plenty about setting up pretty offices, but they don't know much about paper flow. Without meaning to, they make the people secondary to the traffic flow, secondary to the paper flow, and secondary— ultimately—to the cash flow.

▷ A Bad Example: Is This Your Office?

Paper comes into your In-Bin (let's say it's on your right). You take a piece of paper out of the bin, put it in front of you, start working—and someone interrupts you. You put the paper down on your left, intending to come back to it later. When you're finally free again, you bring it back in front of you. If it's not handled by quitting time, you put it back in the In-Bin on your right.

All day this paper has crossed back and forth in front of you, yet you don't feel like you've accomplished

51

anything. There *is* a connection between the way the paper moves and the amount of accomplishment you feel. When paper moves around uselessly, you feel useless at the end of the day.

▷ One Simple Secret to Organizing

It's much easier to rearrange your furniture than to continue working in a difficult environment. In the next section you will learn how to set up your office to circulate paper around you—from your In-Bin, through your work area, and out again.

Your first step is not necessarily to reduce the amount of paper in your office (that comes later, if at all); it's to get paper moving around you in a circle, and to use your furniture to support that circular flow.

But first, here's some background about furniture and how it can cause disorganization.

◁ How Your Furniture is Causing U to Become Disorganized

Ever since offices were invented, we have been squirming around blocky furniture, cranky file drawers, tight knee space, balky chairs, and worse. Then ergonomics came in; we are now more health-conscious as far as our chairs and keyboards are concerned, but we still have to work with angular desks. Even if your desk is curved, the various pieces of furniture in the rest of your office are probably arranged in a square or rectangular pattern.

Humans don't adapt well to squares and angles. Look at the human body and see how it actually moves: Stretch both your arms out straight in front of you, then swing them wide until they are sticking out to the sides. Notice that your hands are describing a semicircle in the air.

Someday all office furniture will be semicircular, reflecting how humans are really built. Until then, paper needs hands and arms to move it along, so let's rearrange your furniture to match your semicircular arm movements and get your paper to flow more smoothly around you.

◁ How to Get Your Furniture to Organize U

The best arrangement for most offices is three contiguous work surfaces. Think of sitting inside a big U-shaped furniture configuration. Not L-shaped or J-shaped: those don't mimic your arm movements as well as a U-shape does.

Your U-shape can be made up of three tables, a desk with a return (side piece) and a credenza; a desk and credenza with one lateral file; or many other options. The goal is to create a three-part semicircle of work surfaces. If you aren't ready to buy new furniture, look around and see what you've got that you can use. A parson's table? A folding table? A door on two file cabinets is still a good option—just multiply the door by three and the file cabinets by six. Remember, three pieces of furniture in a U-shape around you is the goal.

If you are stuck working in a small cubicle with only one countertop, you might think you can't make a three-sided U-shape, but you can. Put a short bookcase beside you (they're only 10"-12" deep) and two short file cabinets behind you.

If there's not enough room, ask for shelves to hang on two of the walls behind and beside your work surface. (I know one woman who worked at her kitchen table and used an ironing board beside her and two file cabinets behind her.)

Keep working at it until you have a U-shaped work surface at hand height. Don't leave any gaps that paper could fall into.

Because the U-shaped work surface emulates the motions we make with our arms, this arrangement will help you to:

- reach everything on your work surface easily

- swivel smoothly from one project to another

- minimize the time it takes to recoup from an interruption

  (and, *drum roll please*, the secret bonus:)

- keep people out of your work area because it wraps around you. Ta-daa!

IF YOU DON'T WANT YOUR FURNITURE MOVED AROUND

You are doomed. Just kidding! Really though, furniture rearrangement is *such* an integral part of improving paper flow that to refuse the idea is to throw away one of the most powerful tools I have to offer you. Are you sure you don't want to read just a little further before you make up your mind?

▷ The Geographical Distortion Theory

The Geographical Distortion Theory says that the farther apart two people work, the more likely it is that paper traveling between them will get disorganized. Faxes and e-mail were supposed to reduce this problem, but humans will always be humans, and paper will always move from hand to hand more than any other way.

And no, there will never be any such thing as a paperless office. Working in office without paper would be like swimming in a pool without water. What would be the point?

▷ How to Stash Your Trash

Even the location of your trash can is important: Think about how many times a day you bend, twist, stretch, and reach to throw away trash. Does your back hurt? The location of your trash can may be part of the problem.

Sit back in your chair, crumple some scratch paper, and let it drop from your hand. That's where your trash can belongs. If its new location interferes with your traffic pattern, of course you can make adjustments. Just be sure it's easy to toss trash from your chair to the can without bending, leaning or stretching all day long.

▷ Don't Trip Up the Traffic

Observe the traffic flow in your office. Where are people going to walk? Here's an easy way to look at it: Draw a map of your office as it is now. Include all of the desks, tables, and chairs.

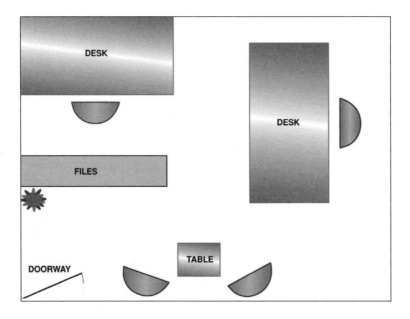

Now draw lines (curvy lines, if necessary) from the door to the chair, and from the door to your desk, showing how people walk. These are your current traffic patterns.

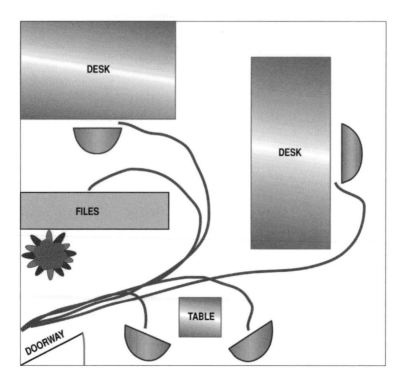

When people can't get where they're going easily, they get frustrated and, eventually, resentful. The more resentful *they* get, the more files and paperwork *you'll* lose. And guess where they'll leave stuff? You got it—on the catchers between your desk and the door.

Now that you've seen how the traffic flows, mark the locations of the electrical outlets, computers, calculators and so forth on your drawing. Do you see any conflicts?

> ***When the traffic flow isn't smooth and natural, people get irritated because they have to navigate around furniture dozens of times each day.***

Well-meaning people will tell you it doesn't matter where the outlets are because you can always add power strips and extension cords. You will create more problems than you solve, however, if people keep tripping over cords or if the power strips become overloaded. Take it easy on your power strips, and situate your furniture so that power cords don't cross the traffic flow.

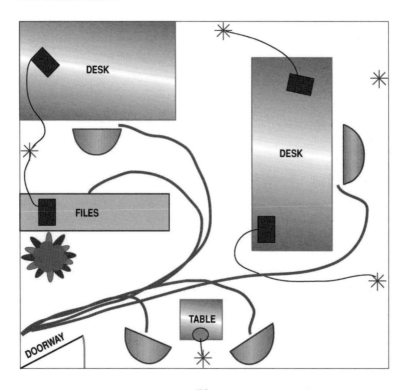

Also, since some cords are phone and data cables—which have their own limitations—you can create even bigger problems if you're not careful. (What is the sound of one network crashing?)

ELECTRICAL OUTLETS AND TRAFFIC FLOW OPTIONS

If you are remodeling, have your electrician pull both data and phone wires into one central floor outlet, and make sure they put a cover on it. This gives you much more flexibility when it comes to locating furniture.

Just be sure the cover is flush with the floor so no one will trip on it.

▷ Your Ideal Furniture Arrangement

Now draw the fabulous new furniture arrangement you'd love to have, using the three-sided, U-shaped configuration. Remember to take those electrical outlets and natural traffic paths into account!

Once you have your new plan, go ahead and rearrange your furniture accordingly. You may have to buy another piece to get the desired U-shape, but you will recoup that money many times over in improved efficiency and saved time—not to mention lower doctor bills.

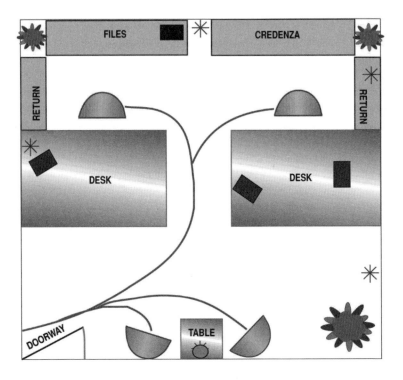

> ## Furniture Arrangement Tips

- Be aware of traffic patterns and don't block them.

- Move your furniture until you can sit in the middle of your U-shaped configuration and reach all three surfaces without leaning or reaching.

- Don't sit with your back to a door—new projects might sneak into your In-Bin when you're not looking!

- Don't place the computer monitor so that it faces a window, or you'll end up with a glare on the screen.

- Be sure you've left enough room to open your desk drawers *and* push your chair back. Usually forty to forty-five inches is about right for pushback. Measure from the edge of the desk (at your belly) to the wall or furniture *behind* your chair.

- Put at least one side of your U-shaped work area near the door so people can drop things off without invading your space.

- Make sure you can reach your In-Bin from your chair without standing up.

- Avoid gaps between furniture that allow paper to "drip down" into the cracks.

ARE YOU A TRASH MONSTER?

If you work at Chateau Debris with tons of junk all over the place, of course you can't move the furniture yet. Here are three options:

1. Organize your paperwork first; then move the furniture (this works best for Linears ✔).

2. *Chunk* huge stacks of paper into boxes indiscriminately and get them away from you (maybe out into the hall?) in one swell foop. Move the furniture into place. Then move the boxes back in and organize the papers as you take them out.

Chunk: to move large clumps of paper without going through every single piece.

✋ Spatials are especially willing to chunk without sorting, because they love the instant open space!

---

3. *Semi-Chunk:* move the stacks out carefully. Label them as you go—verbs are best. (For example, "Input to mailing," "Put in bookcase," etc.) Label some stacks with nouns if verbs don't work. This is a temporary situation. Try to keep a good chunking pace going.

When the room is clear enough, rearrange the furniture. After that you can bring the boxes back in.

Number three takes the longest, because you have to go through the stacks twice, but it's less traumatic for Sparklebrains ☀ and Visuals ☻.

Chapter 6
Nine Supplies You Need to Get Organized

What supplies will you need to get organized? Here's the list for every Organizing Style. You can buy these the same day you start organizing, or weeks in advance.

▽   **The Supply List that Will Save You**

1.   One box of large plastic trash bags in the yard-cleaning size. Be sure they're heavy (0.9 to 1.0 mil). Thin bags will have you swearing when they tear. How many will you need? Between one and six bags for each person getting organized.

2.   One box of manila folders. They come in two sizes: letter and legal. Use the one that fits your filing cabinets.

3.   One box of variously colored file folders. (Get the paper folders, not the plastic ones.) You can buy 100 folders in five colors for about $10, or you can get fluorescent folders in packs of 12 or so for about $7.

You'll need between 15 and 50 folders (not boxes of folders) for each person getting organized.

4. One set of thin-tipped markers for labeling file folders. I like the Vis-a-Vis brand best for this task.

5. Post-Its—how did we ever run an office without them? Buy several sizes and several colors (think about which colors *inspire you to work*, not which colors you *like*).

6. Several 3"x 5" notepads *or* several hundred 3"x 5" index cards (white) *or* recycled paper (with at least one side blank) and cut into note-sized pieces.

7. Bankers boxes for things waiting to be filed, books to be put away, and so on. How many will you need? They come six or ten to a set; the average office uses one or two sets per person.

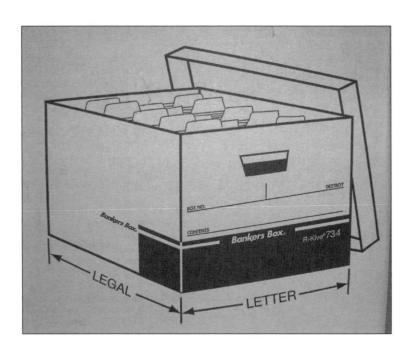

8. A heavy metal standing file for the top of your desk to hold your files in stairstep fashion (about $25.00). Alternative: a plastic shoebox or sweater bin.

9. Plastic shoeboxes and sweater bins. If you can walk through your office easily and your disorganization is restricted to the top of your desk, get three to six of each size. If your office is so full you can barely walk through it and your disorganization spreads to two, three, or more desks and tables, get ten to twelve of each size. You can return what you don't use, but you'll probably use them all.

▷ Supplies to Avoid Buying at All Costs

Before you rush off to buy standard in-baskets or any other traditional desktop containers, read this.

Most people buy their containers from office supply stores, and therein lies the problem. Traditional in- and out-baskets, mail trays, sorters, pen and pencil holders, stacking trays, etc., are all too small.

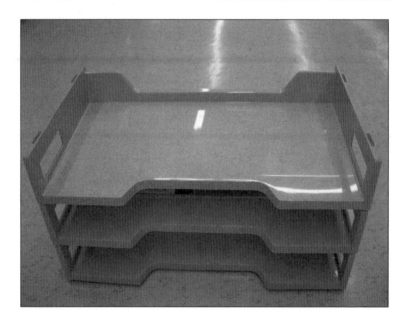

What you need is larger containers. Why? Because you're a modern, forward-thinking, advanced kind of person—and standard containers were designed way back in the 1950s. The typical office today has ten times more paper than offices did then, and that's even before you count the output from the internet and e-mail.

70

When you try to cram today's volumes of paper into those little, old-fashioned in-and-out trays, you might think you're making them look less intimidating, but you're fooling no one. It still looks just like an intimidating amount of stuff crammed into little containers. Besides, it means you'll have to look in even more places to find whatever you're looking for.

CONTAINERS TO MATCH YOUR ORGANIZING STYLE

Visuals 👁: tall containers are bad for you. Once they're full, you won't look down into them, which means you won't see what's inside, which means you won't take the stuff out and work on it.

Spatials ✋: stay away from enclosed containers or any container with rough edges. If you have to reach down into something with sharp edges, you'll stop using it and everything in it. Lots of little containers will also prevent you from reaching in to pull things out: Once stuff is in there, it'll stay there.

Chrons 🕐: you'll do well to use an accordion file, pending file, or any container that has dates or numbers on it.

For you Chrons, large stacked trays will work even better, because they reflect the "strata" of events in your mind. Be sure they are marked with the due date or the date of retrieval though, and make sure the trays are large enough to put your entire hand into.

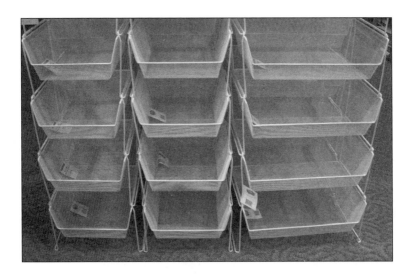

▷ Good Containers, Bad Containers

Sort your stuff first to see how much you have, then evaluate the size of the containers you'll need, and *then* (and only then!) buy the right size containers. True, some stuff may have to sit on the floor for a day or two until you purchase your containers, but consider the alternative: a bunch of small trays overflowing again.

If you want really fancy containers, do your shopping at an antique store or import store. Think about unusual containers—things you don't ordinarily see in an office. You can use big flat baskets, wooden bins, metal trays, ceramic pots, or just about any kind of container, as long as it's big enough.

The best containers have clear, translucent, or mesh sides so you can see into them. If you can't see into them, you won't take stuff out of them.

If you are a Cross-Dominant ✈ you have even more stuff than the average working person. If you think you'll need more containers, buy several extra plastic shoeboxes and sweater bins. They always come in handy.

Don't buy any type of container other than I have recommended here.

Warning! *Do not,* under any circumstances, not even if you're a highly trained organizer, buy any kind of file storage with a covered top. You will organize it nicely with oh-so-pretty folders, close the top, stack things on top of it *just once,* and never open it again. You know I speak the truth!

Chapter 7
Setting the Stage for Getting Organized

*How can you make sure you don't lose impor-
tant papers while you're getting organized?
Should you "clean for the cleaning people?"*

*Use this chapter the same day you start
organizing your office. This is the prepara-
tion—we'll start the step-by-step organizing
process in chapter 8.*

*How long will it take to get organized? There's
no way to predict—everybody's different.*

◁ You Must Have a Central Headquarters

Ask yourself, "What would I miss if I didn't see it for
three days or a week while I'm getting organized?" Go
get a big box and put it on a separate chair, on the floor,
or on an unused desk. Label it, *"Central Headquarters."*

In this Central Headquarters box, put all those things you don't want out of your sight: your urgent papers and projects, your checkbook, appointment calendar, Palm Pilot, Rolodex and all those loose phone numbers. Keeping them in the box will ensure they won't get mixed in with the other stuff we're going to start organizing. Now, if you need to put your hands on something immediately during your office organizing project, you'll find it in your Central Headquarters box.

CENTRAL HEADQUARTERS

Set aside these important items by storing them temporarily in a large box. Try to get this done in less than ten minutes. Go!

- Address book/Rolodex/ frequently-called numbers and recent phone messages

- Calendar/appointment book/ Visor/PDA/Palm Pilot

- Phone (no joke! Or you'll be looking for it when it rings . . .)

- Pager and other electronic devices

- Tape dispenser, stapler, staple remover, letter opener, paper clips

- Marking pens and all the new supplies you just purchased, plus your favorite pens and pencils

- Checkbook

- Bills to be paid this week

- Current paperwork and projects

  . . . and anything else you might need to get your hands on quickly.

▷ How to Keep People Out of Your Stuff

Put this sign on your Central Headquarters box: "DO NOT DISTURB! WET PAINT!" I'm not kidding! If you don't protect your stuff now, you won't find it later. And for some reason, this is a sign that gets people's attention. Who cares if they laugh—at least you'll have achieved your objective: to keep them out of your stuff.

Signs and labels are an important organizing tool: They signify your intentions to everyone, including yourself, and they make things much easy to find later when the smoke clears.

During the time you're getting organized you will naturally have a lot of stuff on the desk, the floor, and even out in the hall. After all, if you're going to make an omelette, you'll be breaking a few eggs.

Labels give your stuff that certain air of authority, which is useful when you want people to leave it alone—or when you want to act like you know what you're doing.

▷ How to Get More Work Surface

No matter which Access Type you are, you'll need a surface to work on. Let's start preparing it now.

➡ Here's What To Do: Clearing the Desktop

1. Make a pile of the remaining papers. The purpose of this is twofold: First, you need to see just how much paperwork (and how many projects) you have in process. Second, it helps to clear off your work surface.

   Make sure you pile up all the remaining papers, whether they are blank or written on. Include those phone numbers you've been meaning to put in your Rolodex, those letters you haven't gotten around to answering, the magazines, the business cards, everything.

And no picking through it just yet—I saw that! Relax. We will be going through it soon, and you don't want to do it twice, do you?

2. Put the pile of papers into a cardboard box. If you have more than one box, stack them on the floor without stopping to sort anything. I know you're itching to get to it, but you won't get the rewards unless you stick with the program. I promise to walk you through it.

3. Now clear your desk of any decorations or whatever else is left: the Gary Larson calendar, pictures, plants, the desk blotter, everything. Put these objects on a windowsill, in another box, or across the room—somewhere completely away from your desk. Clear off your desktop completely.

So here's what we have:

- a box of urgent papers and office tools, labeled Central Headquarters,

- one or more boxes of papers, which we will sort through in a moment, and

- a box of decorations and everything else.

Look at how much paper there is. Intimidating, isn't it? Take a moment to appreciate the sheer quantity of it. (If you find yourself sweating and shaking, calm down. From here on, it hurts a lot less.)

Ah, now, stop picking through it! I saw that! You really are wasting your time, you know, because we're going to go through it together in just a moment.

Now go get a damp paper towel, clean off your desktop, and spend a moment admiring the beauty of it. How long has it been since you've seen it this clean? Or seen it at all?

OK, get ready to start organizing.

Chapter 8
From Here to Efficiency

This is the chapter in which we start organizing your office, step by step. Be sure you've read the prior chapters or you'll have no idea what's going on.

Remember your Work Personality and Access Type? You're going to need them for this section, so if you want a reminder, go back and reread chapter 1.

Starting with this chapter, you will begin to see what I call "Magic Questions." These questions are designed to help you become self-sufficient in organizing. Your answers will tell you what steps to take for your special Organizing Style. The more you practice asking yourself these questions, the easier organizing gets. Eventually, all you will need is the questions—not the whole book.

In fact, there is a summary of the Magic Questions at the end of this book for just that purpose.

◁ Handle Paper Twice: Why Breaking the Rules will Improve Your Results

One of the tips most traditional organizing books repeat is, "handle paper once. Don't put it down until you've taken action on it," they say. I disagree heartily! The concept has intimidated many an innocent person. But take heart! I'll help you find an alternative that will make it all better.

Imagine trying to follow that rule: If you weren't allowed to put things down until you'd finished them, you'd be carrying *all* your paper with you, *all* the time! You might as well never pick up *any* paper, for fear of not being able to put it down. I know I'm pushing it here, but doesn't that sound like your current situation?

If you dread dipping into your In-Bin, maybe it's because this unworkable, *handle-it-once* rule has invaded your brain and created unnecessary panic.

You also can't handle all incoming paper immediately. It's a fantasy, so give it up. It's about as effective as putting a sign outside your work area that says, "Interruption Free Zone." Sure, that would work for a while—about as long as it takes to turn your job into a paycheck-free zone.

Here's A Traditional Organizing Rule That Just Flames Me

"Handle each piece of paper once. Don't put it down until you've taken action on it."

Can't be done! The only paper you can handle once is Kleenex! (OK now, I'm going to ignore that other thought you just had.)

I think what those traditional organizing books meant to say was, "don't put paper down until you've *advanced* it a step." But they didn't say that, so I will. Don't put paper down until you've *advanced* it a step, OK? We'll get to the details shortly. But first, consider this.

▷ When You Can Let Paper Sit

In real life, most paperwork is just started, partially done, still in the thinking stages, needing research, or waiting for information from someone else before you can proceed with it. It's halfway between *done* and *not done*, but we're not taught how to handle these halfway things, and they are the ones that make us feel the guiltiest. *These* are the papers that cover our desks: the semi-completed projects, the *in-progress* items.

If you're not sure of what to do with a certain paper, put it back in your In-Bin to *marinate*. Can you do that? Is it acceptable? Sure, why not? Marinating is a must for paperwork that's not yet ready for action. Think about it: If you tried to process such raw paperwork before it was ready or without knowing the next step, you'd end up having to do it all over again later. So let it marinate.

Marinating is a valid reason for postponement. It's not the same thing as procrastination—not at all. Procrastination is denial and avoidance; marination is purposeful postponement.

Sometimes *all* you know about a certain piece of paper is that you don't know what to do with it. Leave it in your In-Bin to marinate, and you're sure to see it over and over again. Isn't that an easy way to remind yourself to do it?

There's no harm in handling a piece of paper three or four or even more times. Handle paper as often as you need to. Consider the alternative: Trying to finish all your projects at once is like trying to eat all your lunch in one bite.

From now on, we're *purposely* going to avoid finishing paperwork unless it can be done easily in one step (what I call a "one-shot task"). We're going to advance paper only one step at a time. I know; it goes against traditional organizing rules, but that's kind of the point. This way is easier, more convenient, far more productive in the long run, and it will save huge amounts of time. And it works.

◁ Organizing in the Olden Days

When I was an administrative assistant—about 150 years ago—all paperwork was sorted and filed by nouns. When someone received a letter, it was considered *correspondence*, (a noun) whether it required a response or not. When someone had to make copies, they said they had to *Xerox*. Everything was nouns.

▷ The New Terminology

Nouns are still useful to *describe* our To-Dos, but we make them come alive (and motivate ourselves to get things done) when we translate our nouns into verbs. By *verbing*—writing a verb telling us what to do on each task—we advance our work one giant step toward completion. We *file* correspondence; we *copy*, we *e-mail*, we *fax*—all verbs.

▷ How Verbs Can Save You Tons of Time

The most effective way to start organizing is to go through your In-Bin, labeling each piece of paper with a verb. With each one, ask yourself, What is the action I'm going to take with this? Then write your verb on the paper (or on a stickie and attach it to the paper).

Work with just one task at a time. It's tempting to race ahead once you've discovered this verbing trick, but hold steady. Don't move too fast or take shortcuts, or you'll end up right back where you were. We'll do it together, and I'll show you the steps.

This process will move slowly at first, then pick up speed as you get used to it. But there are more steps to come, so take it easy, OK?

➡ Step by Step: Verbing 101

1. Pick up any piece of paper. Just one, please.

2. What is it? Start by describing it with a noun. For example, it's an e-mail.

   But wait! Just because you *received* an e-mail doesn't mean you are going to *respond* with an e-mail. You might respond with a fax, with a phone call, or by deleting the e-mail altogether. So don't automatically verb it *e-mail* just because that's how you *received it*. Think about what you *will* do, not what was done last.

3. Now ask yourself, What is the action to be taken? Listen to your answer—it's a verb, isn't it? For example, let's say you decide to respond by fax; fax is your verb. Write *fax* on the upper right-hand corner of the paper (or on a stickie and attach it to the paper).

Verbing is the easiest shortcut to getting organized, because it cuts to the heart of the matter by simply telling you what your next step is. It also cuts down on time you used to spend remembering—or guessing.

Don't put the paper down until you've finished writing your verb on it; then set it aside. This does not contradict what I wrote earlier, when I cited the traditional rule that says, Don't put it down until you've *handled* it. The new rule is, Don't put it down until you've *verbed* it. (Except, of course, that you *can* put it down if you have to answer a call, go to the bathroom, etc. Just put it down in your In-Bin, which ensures that you'll come across it again when you resume verbing.)

Magic Question #1

"What is the action I need to take with this?"

Always start with this Magic Question.

---

4. Write the verb in the upper right-hand corner of the paper (or wherever you choose, but make sure you write it in the same place every time so it's easy to find).

89

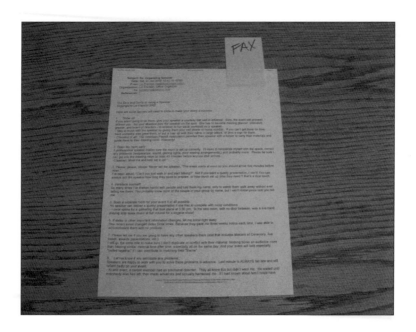

Don't stop to actually *send* the fax now. Remember to focus on one step at a time. Once it's verbed, set it aside and take the next paper from your In-Bin.

5. Verb the next paper and set it aside, then the next, and so on. Don't go past the verb for now. Keep asking and answering the question, What action needs to be taken?

    If you are holding several papers at once, put them down—all except one. Notice whether it's your habit to hold many papers at one time. If so, practice emptying your hands and focusing on one thing at a time until you have written a verb on it. Don't take any action on the paper yet: just verb it, then set it aside. Reduce your stress by focusing on one paper (or set of papers) at a time.

6. When you're ready for a break, set all the verbed papers aside. You now have two stacks: verbed and not verbed.

7. When you're ready for more, resume verbing. With a little practice, every time you pick up a piece of paper, you'll automatically say both the noun and the verb: This is an *e-mail,* and I'm going to respond by *fax.* After a while you'll say just the verb, *fax.*

The point of verbing each piece of paper is to prevent you from reviewing it every time you see it, and saying, What was I going to do with this again? Oh, yeah, now I remember.

When you think of how much time you spend saying that every day, then multiply your answer by the days in a year . . . that's the answer to two questions you've been asking: Where does the time go? and, Why is there so much on my mind?

This verbing may seem like a tiny step now, but it will save you tons of time later on.

Changing nouns to verbs is one of the secret tricks to making paper flow smoothly. The old nouns we used kept things in the past; now verbs move them into the future. Verbs are what motivate us to get things done.

8. Finish verbing your papers without completing any of the tasks on them—unless, of course, they're emergencies. (Definition of emergency: when life or property is in danger.)

   Exception to the rule: if you run across a task that must be done immediately, do it. Otherwise, stick with the program and keep on verbing.

Just a little more on verbing and we'll be moving on.

Notice that when you return to your *verbed* and *not-yet-verbed* stacks, it's easy to see where you left off, by looking at which papers have verbs in the upper right-hand corner.

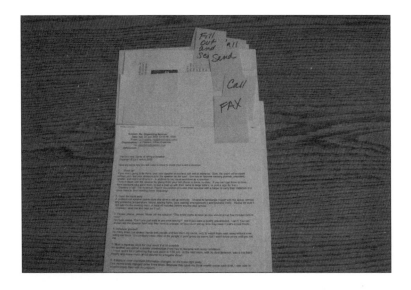

From now on, verb each task as soon as you know the action you need to take. Within a day or two you will start to realize huge time savings because you don't have to go through the same paperwork over and over again.

And from now on, when you see paperwork with a verb on it, you'll know you've completed the first step—identifying the action to be taken.

This verbing process will soon become second nature and will gradually improve your work rhythm. You will be "going with the flow." And this is only the first step.

▷ How to Get Paper to Keep Moving Itself

When choosing your verb, be specific. *Do* is not enough because it's not specific, it's not motivating, and when you see it again, you won't know what kind of action to take.

Besides, everything on your desk is a *do*. (Also not allowed is the word *miscellaneous*, which is Latin for, "Never look at this again.")

Only *you* know which verb will work best, which one motivates *you*. For example, you might assume that *fax* is most effective—after all, that's what you need to do, isn't it? But if you hate faxing (yet you still need to do it), pick a different verb—one that you like better. How about, *fun faxing, faxing for dollars*, or some other phrase that motivates you? It sounds silly, but it works!

Sometimes longer, more specific verb phrases work better than just one verb. Give yourself as much help as you can to get the ball rolling.

Don't be afraid to use five words instead of one, especially if it will save you time and help you focus later, when you really need it.

Example:

Short 'n' Vague:	Specific 'n' Longer:
E-mail	E-mail for meeting date
Call	Call for input to agenda

▷ **Why Your Words Are So Important**

Use your own verbs and no one else's. I can't tell you how many times I've organized an office for one business partner while the other sat nearby and answered questions on their behalf. Just trying to be helpful, you know.

The problem is, Person A's memory is *not* going to be triggered later by the verb Person B chooses.

Don't let any organizing book, helper, neighbor, spouse, friend, or *anyone* change the verbs you decide on. We are setting up a system for *you* to find things easily later on, based on *your* Inner Organizer's wording. If you don't use your *own* verbs, your system won't work for you. Period.

It might take several tries to settle on a motivating verb.

Visuals 👁, Synesthetes 𝔖 and Cross-Dominants ✈, try closing your eyes as you think of your verb, to help you minimize distractions.

Here's Another Traditional Organizing Rule That Just Flames Me

"Make files with these labels."

Many traditional organizing books tell you which action words, or verbs, to use. For example, they suggest that you label things "To call," "To fax," "To copy," etc.

I think they are missing the most important part: the part that makes (or breaks) a good organizing system—that words reflect the way you access. If your system is based on your special verbs, words and labels, it will continue to be meaningful to you. Otherwise, it's just generic advice from yet another organizing book.

▷ How to Find Your Stuff When You Need It

Listen to your verb as you say it—not just the word itself, but the way you use it. For example, do you *call, contact,* or *phone*? Do you *copy, make copies,* or *photocopy*? Be sure to label your papers with the exact verb (or verb phrase) that comes out of your mouth. Otherwise, you will have trouble finding things later. (Odd, but true!)

▷ The Advantages of Verbing

Verbing your papers gives you a head start and a place to start. In addition, it . . .

- gives you a reminder that an action still needs to be taken

- reminds you which action to take

- keeps you focused on your current activity, while still allowing you to take short detours and handle interruptions

- reduces your resistance to working (because you wrote it, and since you trust your own handwriting, you're more inclined to follow through willingly).

Verbing your paperwork is only the first step to getting it under control, but it's a very big step—in fact, it's the key to the rest of the steps. Now you can speed up or slow down your pace without losing momentum or forgetting where you left off. You can pause, handle an interruption, and find your place again, without freaking out because things weren't finished before you set them down.

Best of all, even if you drop your papers all over the floor, you'll know what you have to do just by looking at the verbs. So simple!

Chapter 9
Chaos Control: What to Do with All That Pending Paperwork

> *What should you do with all your verbed tasks waiting to be done? How can you keep your desk clear? When is all this stuff going to get finished?*

◁ **An Introduction to Controlling the Piles**

Everyone knows how to throw things away, and everyone knows how to file. Some people may *not* file, but they know how. Filing and tossing aren't the major reasons people call me; they call me because they can't figure out where to put all that paperwork that's **pending**.

In this chapter you will learn what to do with your pending paperwork. We're going to group them by verbs into new containers called Control Folders. These folders will take on the job of controlling all the bits of paperwork until you can move forward on them. And they are temporary, so if you don't like them you can change them easily.

If you didn't finish verbing all your paperwork, it's OK. You can finish later. There will always be more coming in; you know there will!

◁ Step by Step, Getting Your Paperwork Under Control

Control Folders contain work in progress; work that's somewhere between *done* and *not done*. They hold everything from fledgling ideas, to work that's marinating, to work that's waiting to be started.

When you use Control Folders you can see all the things you have to do at once, and your desk will still be neat. These folders work *with* your verbs to do much of your organizing for you.

WHAT CONTROL FOLDERS DO FOR YOU

Your new Control Folders show you Visually ☻, Spatially ✋, and Chronologically ⏱ how much work you have to do and where to find it.

With Control Folders, your work is still only partially done, but you're far better off than you were before: Your desk looks better, the pressure is off, and the mess is gone—but your papers are still accessible.

➡️ ### Start Here to Set Up Your Control Folders

1. Pick up any piece of paper you've already verbed.

2. Read your verb out loud—this fixes it firmly in your mind.

3. Look at the colored folders you bought. What colors do you have?

If you're a Linear ✔, a Chron 🕒, or both, skip steps 4 through 7, but be sure to pick it up again at step 8. Everyone else, do all the steps.

---

4. If you're a synesthete 𝔇, close your eyes and say the verb out loud again. What color do you see in your mind's eye? Notice the question is not what you *think,* but what you *see.*

101

5.   Your folders have left, middle and right tabs. If you're a synesthete 𝔶, close your eyes again. Which tab did you see? Say it out loud, then open your eyes. Your goal is to settle on a color, a side (left, middle, or right tab), and a verb (or a phrase that starts with a verb.)

6.   Now pick up a folder that matches what you saw in your mind's eye.

Linears ✔ will see the same color with their eyes open as when they are closed—just another example of their dependability—and Chrons 🕒 don't care about colored folders. Both of them will do better with due dates on their labels instead of verbs.

---

7.   Using your markers, print your verb on the label.

Make sure it's the same verb you said earlier—this is important! Print the same verb *again* in big letters across the bottom front of the folder to increase **findability.**

Note: If you hate the idea of separating your projects into Control Folders by verbs, don't do it!

Instead, go directly to chapter 12 and read about how to use Project Folders and bins. Try them instead of Control Folders.

---

8. When settling on your folder color, don't strive to choose by meaning—like red for *urgent.* Meaning doesn't have anything to do with it. Say only the color you saw with your eyes closed. This is what accessing your Inner Organizer is all about!

   Your answer may surprise you, and you might have to practice this exercise until you get used to it. Relax, close your eyes and stay with it until you see something that *looks* right to you. That'll be your best color choice. If you don't see a particular color after several tries, move on to another verb. You can always come back again later.

9. Go through the rest of your verbed papers, making Control Folders that support your verbs. Put the verbed papers into the corresponding folders.

    Note: Do *not* start off making a bunch of folders based on what you *think* your verbs and colors should be. Doing what you think you *should* is using your *Outer Organizer.* This exercise works by tapping into your *Inner Organizer* and finding associations (not meanings) you didn't know you had.

    Follow the directions of the verbs you've already established; *then* make the folders.

WHEN YOU WRITE ON YOUR FOLDER LABELS

Use thin-tipped markers for your Control Folder labels. Regular pens will result in writing that's too small to read from more than six feet away, which will become necessary under certain extreme circum-stances—like age. Felt pens that are too large will make your letters run together.

👁 𝔇 Hand write your labels in clear, colorful letters. Your Control Folders must be easy to see.

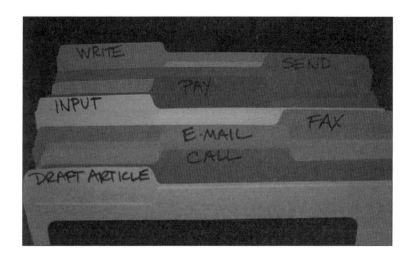

Keep your new Control Folders separate, and keep channeling your active work into them.

If you already had an action system or some other kind of organizing folders, take the contents out, toss the folders, and put the contents into your new Control Folders based on your new verbs. Why can't you keep the old folders? Because the labels weren't motivating you to do the work inside them. The papers got stale, didn't they? That's why you're reading this book, right?

Eventually you can channel papers directly from your In-Bin to your Control Folders without stopping to verb them. Just be sure they won't get knocked over, scattering the contents and making you do all that work again.

▷ Is It Working Yet?

You will know if your Control Folders motivate you if you find yourself opening them and doing the work inside. If you're not opening them, if you hate them, or if you find you're not using them, they're not motivating you. Improve them by changing to more appropriate colors and verbs.

❖ Fooling Yourself for Fun and Profit

When I first started this business back in 1979, we didn't have personal computers. Every time I had to write a proposal, I had to type it from scratch, and I *hate* typing proposals from scratch! Like a child with schoolwork, I always left proposals until Sunday night and then complained.

I decided to group my proposals into a folder so I could find them easily, thinking this would get me to do them sooner. I named the folder "Proposals." Of course, nothing changed. The folder sat there until the last possible minute, just like before.

Then I stumbled onto verbing things. Thinking I was brilliant, I changed the folder label to, "Write Proposals." But I got the same result—no production and ruined Sunday evenings.

Finally I decided things had to change. Why, I asked myself, am I doing this? The answer was simply money. So I threw away the old folder, got out a nice new one, and drew big green dollar signs all over it—front, back, label, everywhere.

It worked! It motivated me to open the folder and do the work inside while there was still plenty of time.

Pick a title that *motivates* you to do your work in a timely manner. That's the whole point.

𝔇 Use colors, ideas and verbs that you see in your mind's eye, and your folders will work for you.

Be careful! Several of my clients have tried using titles they hate to represent hateful tasks. For example, one woman made a bright red folder called "Stupid Budget Work I Hate," because she hates red. My response was, "Will that color and title motivate you to reach for that folder and do the work inside?" Nope. She changed it.

If your folder doesn't motivate you, change the color, the verb, or both.

WHEN COLORS BECOME EMOTIONAL

The big rival college football teams in the San Francisco Bay Area are Stanford and the University of California at Berkeley. Stanford's colors are red and white, Cal's are blue and gold. When I organize an office for someone who went to Cal, they won't let me use red folders. Stanford alumni don't like blue lettering on a gold folder. This is emotional stuff, folks! The reasons don't matter; the results do.

◁ How Being Silly Can Get You Organized

Silly folder names can be very effective. A word, picture, or phrase that makes it fun to pull the folder and look inside will work better than just some plain old verb.

Here are some real life Control Folder titles my clients have come up with:

- "My A** Is Grass" (I'll get in trouble if I don't do these)

- "Avoid Financial Disaster" (Pay bills on time)

- "Fishy Business" (Manuals on how to set up the office aquarium)

- "If I Don't Read This No One Will Die" (Reading that can wait)

If your verb phrase makes you laugh, you know you have an excellent motivator!

One client used an exclamation point on one folder, a question mark on another, and nothing else—no words at all. I asked him if he'd remember what they were. He said, very enthusiastically, "Sure! The exclamation point folder is stuff to take home, and the question mark folder is stuff to bring back to the office!"

We tested it over time and it worked: He opened the folders, did the work, and the papers ended up where they needed to go.

Feel free to expand on this system. After all, it's yours!

◁ Where to Keep Your Controlled Paper

Use a heavy metal *standing file* with a slanted base for your Control Folders, or use a plastic box (but make sure you have enough files to keep it from falling over.) Either container allows you to see all your verbs at once, which is the whole, big, entire point.

Also, the large verb labels allow you to review what you have to do at a glance, without re-reading every single piece of paper every single day.

Keep your Control Folders in a holder (henceforth, your *folder holder*) on top of your desk, on the credenza behind you, or beside you where you can reach them easily.

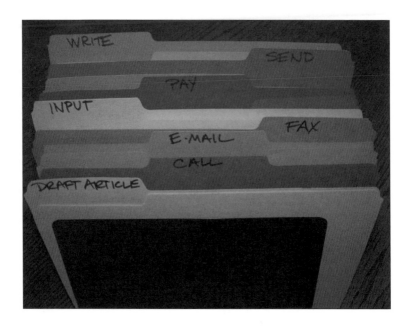

Just make sure you don't have to stand up or reach too far to get them. Keep them super-convenient. You'll be moving paper in and out frequently, so make them easy to use.

Don't put your Control Folders inside a drawer, no matter how tempted you may be. Drawers are storage for noun folders that require no further action. If you put your verbed papers or Control Folders out of sight, your To-Dos will never get To-Done! Keep them where you can see them, especially you Visuals 👁.

▷ How to Handle Evolving Paperwork

If you are like most people, your Control Folders will evolve and change. Let them! If you want to add more Control Folders, feel free to do so at any time.

If, after some time, you find you are not using a certain folder, eliminate it or let the contents marinate in your In-Bin even longer. Pay attention though—there may be a useful clue here. When you are not using one of the folders, remember, it's because the label doesn't mean anything special to you, so re-do it.

Learn to distinguish between files that you don't use often ("Draft annual budget," "Write the Great American Novel," "Compile Nobel speech," etc.), and files you use daily ("Call," "e-mail," "Fax"). Keep the most-used folders closest.

▷ The Advantages of Being a Control Freak

Your colorful Control Folders offer many advantages. Just give them a try and you'll enjoy all these terrific benefits:

- Control Folders are a great way to empty your In-Bin quickly and easily. You'll get credit for being organized (when all you've done is move things into folders), because your desk will look so much neater. You'll also be more willing to work when you can put things aside until you have time to do them.

- Control Folders help keep different activities separate. Emptying the In-Bin is no longer mixed with actually doing work. Attempting both of these activities at once can fry the little circuits between the left and right sides of your brain.

- Control Folders give you a middle ground between work that's done and work that's not, which gives you a greater sense of accomplishment—and a viable method of postponement!

- Control Folders stimulate memory visually, which is great for Sparklebrains ☀, Cross-Dominants ✔, and Visuals 👁. They're also quite a conversation piece, especially if they're fluorescent, in which case you Visuals 👁 will need extra aspirin!

- Control Folders are motivating because of their colors and their verbs.

- They channel the paper flow from your In-Bin into a quiet "backwater" until it's time to bring them out again and work on them. They hold *later* work without confusing it with *sooner* work. You'll get to them in your own time, rather than having to rush, even when your In-Bin is overflowing.

- They help you find any paper on your desk easily. Just ask yourself, What was the action I was going to take? Then look in the corresponding Control Folder.

- They're customized by you, for you, so you're sure to stay interested.

- You can pull a folder toward you, work on it, and put it back without losing your work pace—or your mind. (This is especially important to Cross-Dominants ✈ and Spatials ✌.)

- You can watch your progress more easily, and you can report what's finished more effectively, because the bulkiness of each folder shows the amount of work you have left to do. They also indicate which work is getting backlogged: they're the fullest folders.

- They help you to sleep better at night because you know things are grouped and retrievable, not scattered all over your desk. Your work is safely tucked away, awaiting your attention.

◁ What To Do When Your Workload Overflows

Let your Control Folders fatten up for now. It's a temporary condition. They'll show you how much stuff you've got, and which categories are the largest and most impending. Let them get as big as they want to. If they look like they're going to explode, set them on the floor, put them in a box, put a rubber band around them, stack them on a shelf, or set them aside in some other way, but keep them close enough to reach.

The point here is to allow the stuff in them to build up so you can see how much you have to deal with.

Your fullest Control Folders will probably be these:

- Call

- Read

- File

- Input to database

When verbed papers overflow a Control Folder, grab some large baskets or bins and move the papers into them, one verb per bin. I call these bins, *Holding Tanks*, because they hold stuff until you're ready to deal with it. Label your Holding Tanks with the appropriate verbs and set them aside.

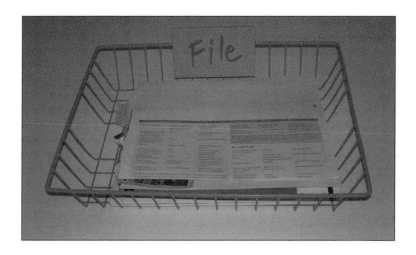

The best Holding Tanks are mesh baskets or translucent plastic tubs because you can see into them, they hold a lot, your labels will show through (they won't fall off if you put them on the inside), and they're cheap.

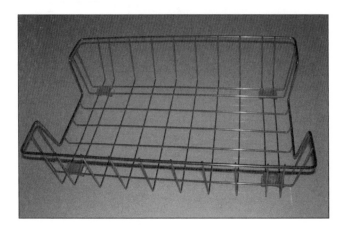

Don't use huge plastic bins, because once they're full, they are extremely hard to move.

Do *not* use tall, skinny plastic boxes that close at the top. They're not big enough to allow your paperwork to expand, and the top will keep you from opening the box and taking work out.

WHEN DO YOU *DO* ALL THIS STUFF YOU'VE BEEN HOLDING?

- ✈ When you have a helper (Saturdays are good for this)

- ✈ When you are on hold (now you'll have something to do with those otherwise wasted minutes!)

- 👁 When you start looking for things that went into the Holding Tanks

- 🕐 Periodically (Once a month, twice a quarter, etc.)

  Should you schedule half an hour a day for this, two hours a week for that? Sure, but it will work only if you are a Chron 🕐!

Keep your Holding Tanks within reach of your chair. Make sure you can toss papers into them easily without standing up, leaning too far, or crossing the room. Keep them either on a shelf (the lowest level of your bookcase?), or on the floor (as long as they are not obstructing the traffic flow.)

Remember to label your bins with *motivating* verbs. If they don't motivate you, change them until they do. The point is to find out how much stuff you have and what you have to do about it, and then motivate yourself to do it.

❖ A Story About Too Darn Much Paper

One of my clients had filled her office with typical office supply store containers. They were too small to hold her stuff, and her office was laid out in such a way that paper got stuck in a lot of "backwaters." The combination of these two problems told me I had to show her how much paper she was dealing with, and fast!

As she verbed her categories, we separated them into large bins: "Read," "File," "Input to computer," etc. After she regained consciousness and saw how much stuff she had, we bought Holding Tanks in sizes to match. They were big enough to bathe in!

When she realized how much paper she had, she was ready to let go of a lot of stuff, and hired a high-school helper to go through the rest with her.

As the old joke goes, "You can't have everything—where would you put it?"

◁ Partners in Slime: To Share or Not to Share?

Can Control Folders be shared? Not unless you enjoy freaking out! No two people have the same projects, priorities or preferences. No two people will see the same colors in their mind's eye. Even Siamese twins aren't always pulling in the same direction. (And you think *you're* stressed!) Sharing Control Folders will only lead to arguments starting with the words, "Well, *you* should . . ." Stick with your own folders, colors, and verbs and let other people choose theirs.

Desdemona can have folders marked "Buy," "Call," "Decide," "Fax" and "Write," while Sven, who has exactly the same job description, might label his, "Errands," "Phone," "Make decisions," "To be faxed," and "Send a note." Differing labels don't hurt anyone, nor do they cause separation anxiety. On the other hand, forcing everyone to use the same colors and labels *will* cause an office rebellion. (You think I'm kidding? Just try it!)

Work gets done better, faster, *and* cheaper when everyone is in charge of their own stuff and organizes it according to their special Organizing Style.

▷ Your Word is Gospel

Nobody is allowed to put stuff into your Control Folders but you. Some people will try to sneak paper into them to see if you're paying attention or because they want your job. Then they will ask you innocently, "You didn't see that memo? I put it on your desk." Liars.

Don't fall for it! Be sure you see *everything* before it goes into *any* of your Control Folders. Here's how: tell everyone that from now on, anything new goes into your In-Bin and nowhere else. Keep your Control Folders beside you or behind you where a casual intruder can't get into them easily. Get snarky about this, because it matters.

◁ What to Do When Your To-Dos are Coming Due

When you run across papers and projects that have a due date, verbing is not enough. You need to take one more step. Ask yourself, *When* does this have to be done? Then attach a stickie with the verb *and the due date* on it.

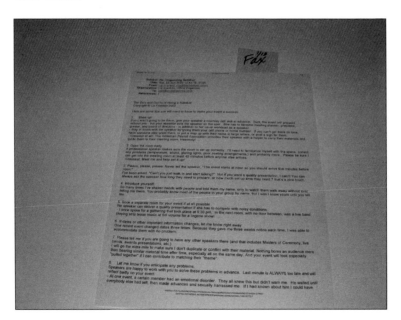

Magic Question #2

"When does this have to be done?"

When something must happen by a certain date or time, flag it with a stickie, leave it out where you can see it, enter it into your calendar, or all three.

➡ Here's What To Do, Step-By-Step, When You Encounter a Dated Item

1. Put down everything else you're holding and focus on that one paper.

2. Always start by asking the first Magic Question first: What *action* must I take with this? Find your verb and get it settled in your mind.

3. Now ask yourself the second Magic Question, *When* must this action take place? Figure out the due date or assign one.

4.   Attach a stickie upside down and backwards to the *side* of the paper so it stands out like a flag and catches your eye. Write the due date and the action verb on it in large, simple print.

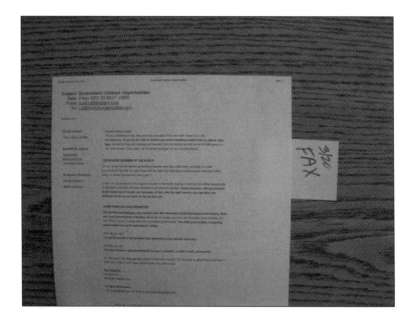

5.   Enter the item into your calendar, Palm Pilot, Visor, or computer. (More is better here.)

Don't worry about duplication. Your choice is to keep everything on your mind, or to store them in several places so they pop up and remind you.

If you think that *still* won't be enough, write an additional note and bury it halfway into the papers in your In-Bin—you *will* run across it again later and it will remind you.

Just don't put the only reminder completely out of sight (like deep inside a Holding Tank) where it will never be seen again.

6. Now put the verbed, dated and stickied paper into the appropriate Control Folder with the flag showing so it will catch your eye.

Your overall challenge is to learn the best way to attract your own attention, and to set things up *now* so they'll alert you *later* when you need them.

➡ HOW TO GET MORE LEISURE TIME

Practice getting ahead of the game by putting *early* due dates on things, by scheduling *too much* time for appointments, and by *overestimating* the time it will take to complete projects.

Haven't you been wondering when you'll get everything done? Well, this is your lucky day! The answer lies in overestimating the amount of time things will take, *consistently and on purpose.* Soon you'll have excess time on your hands on a regular basis. Try it; it works! P.S. If doubling the time doesn't work, try tripling it. Yes, you'll know that you've done it, but it still works!

▷ When One To-Do Has More Than One Due Date

Let's say you're looking at a seminar brochure and you've decided you want to attend. The verb, *attend* doesn't really motivate you, does it? It's not specific, it doesn't give you much information about the steps to take, nor does it say *when* you must take them.

Let's break it down: What are the actions you'll take between now and the time you walk into the seminar? Think about it a step at a time, working backwards.

- I must attend the seminar—but before that

- I must send the check—but before that

- I must fax or e-mail my registration or register on line—but before that

- I must get permission, if necessary, to take time off—but before that

- I must set aside the date—but before that

- I must know the date of the seminar.

Rather than trying to write all that in correct priority order the first time around, let's look at a new, more forgiving method. I call it **Backwardsing Up.**

Take a piece of paper and start at the bottom of the page. Write your goal first, then note the rest of the steps working upwards instead of down. Next to each step, note the due date if you know it.

After writing each step, ask yourself, What must I do before that? Move up a couple of lines and write your answer.

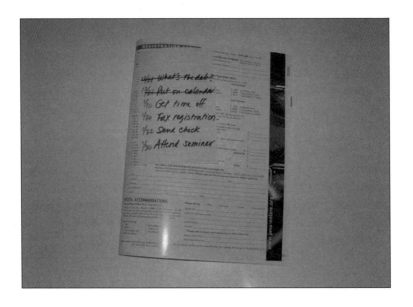

You get bonus points for leaving lots of space between each step. This trick comes in handy if you think of something else to add, but it makes sense even without that, because it makes your list easier to read. It also gets around the traditional organizing rule that you must list your To-Dos in priority order. Hogwash.

Backwardsing Up is a very easy way to plan. It helps you figure out what you need to do between now and the final due date, and it eliminates the need to keep all the steps in your head. It's also the easiest way I know of to end up with a list in priority order without straining your brain in the process.

Backwardsing Up will open your eyes to just how many steps you *really* have to complete. It teaches you to plan more realistically. (Did you know one of the most common reasons for disorganization is unrealistic time estimates?)

Soon all your To-Dos (and the extent to which you have over-obligated yourself!) will snap into focus, and your time estimates will become realistic.

Magic Question #3

"What must I do before that?"

Backwardsing Up is a very effective technique to apply to any task. Grab a piece of paper and start at the bottom, writing your goal. Above that, write what you think you must do to achieve the goal. Then ask yourself, What must I do before that? And before that? When you've run out of *before that's*, you've arrived at the first thing you have to do. Put that one at the top of the page—at the "end" of your backwards list.

▷ **Latering a To-Do**

Sometimes, when you are emptying your In-Bin, verbing your papers, and Backwardsing Up to get the due dates right, you will run across things that aren't due yet. There's no point forcing yourself to work on them today; you've got lots of other stuff that has to come first.

Stop saying, I've got to get all this stuff done today. Instead, look at one task at a time and ask yourself, How long can I put this off without causing a problem? Then label it with that date.

To catch your attention later, put the Backwards Upped lists and papers back in your In-Bin where you'll see them over and over, or put them in the appropriately-verbed Control Folder with the stickies flagging you with the date.

GASP! Put them off? Put them back?! Can you believe an organizer is making this suggestion? Yup, because it works far better than the old alternative, which is stress, overload, and guilt.

It works, it doesn't hurt anyone, and it's a whole lot more realistic than blaming yourself for not finishing everything every day. Too many people allow others to set the pace for them. Who knows better than you do how much work you can handle?

Magic Question #4

"How long can I put this off without causing a problem?"

Extend the date as far out as you can. Write it on a stickie, stick it on the paperwork, and put it somewhere that it will catch your attention.

👁 Place it in such a way that you'll *see* it

✋ Place it *where* you will reach for it

🕐 Place it so that it will get your attention *when* you need it

Traditional organizing books tell you to get things done as *soon* as you can—but you've tried that. It doesn't work, does it?

Besides, you have way too much to do, less and less time in which to do it, and enough pressure without adding more.

So put things off as long as you can. It work, it doesn't hurt anyone, and it's a big relief.

▷ Soonering an To-Do

Afraid you might miss a due date? You're probably right! To avoid this problem, assign a due date that's *sooner* than necessary. You'll see it before it's due, you won't panic, and you'll still have extra time in which to get it done.

For example, if today is the first of the month and an item is due on the 15th, mark it, "Due the 12th" to give yourself a little leeway. Most people would mark it, "Due the 15th" or maybe, "Due the 14th"—but not *you*! You are learning how much work you *really* have to do, so you're planning more and more appropriately, aren't you? To get ahead, cut yourself extra slack by planning ahead.

Stop trying to get everything on your desk done every day. There's really no need, and such an unrealistic approach causes an unbelievable amount of stress. Just set things up with visible date stickies in plenty of time, and you'll get them done—just not today.

> *I have a mantra that gets me through the tough times. When I'm looking at a huge pile of To-Dos and thinking, I can't get all of this done today, I just remind myself that it doesn't all __have__ to be done today.*

131

Chapter 10
How to Get the Help You Need

How much work is too much? Which items can you delegate? How can you store tasks until they are delegated? How can you get them to your helpers in the most effective manner? What helpers?

Now you're beginning to understand. You realize you've agreed to do waaaaay too much work—not to mention the additional projects you keep assigning yourself. Congratulations! You figured it out, and not a moment too soon!

Did you know, some people think they will never die as long as they still have work to do? "I can't die," they tell me. "I'm not finished!" These people make sure their desks are always full.

If the sheer quantity of your workload can no longer be denied, and you feel like pulling your hair out, stop a moment and take heart. It's time to admit there's no way you can do it all alone. You're going to need either more people to help you or less work to do.

How can you get help? Let's go back to nouns and verbs for a moment. Remember, nouns are for things that require no action; verbs are for things that *do* require action. But some verbs work better when you turn them into *proper* nouns—people's names. When should that happen? Whenever you're up to your ears in To-Dos and you could use help.

◁ The Secret to Delegating: Naming Names

Delegate some of your load (especially you Cross-Dominants ✈, please!) by turning your verbs into proper nouns.

For example, "Give to Griselda" starts with a verb. (Whenever your verb is "give to," you're on the verge of delegating.) Make a folder labeled "Griselda" (turn the verb into a proper noun), put the paperwork in it and presto! You've delegated!

When people see a folder with their name on it, they're anxious to pick it up and look inside.

▷ When No One Can Do it But You

Look at one of your too-tall stacks of work. Then ask yourself, Who else can do it besides me? Listen carefully to your answer.

You might say, Nobody. I have to do it myself. OK, maybe that's true—and maybe it isn't. If you think it is, apply a stickie with your *own* name, the verb and the due date. (When one of my helpers sees a stickie that says "Liz call March 3," she's not likely to pick it up and do it herself.)

If someone else *can* do the task (and especially if you don't *want* to do it—hee hee!), put their name on a stickie along with the verb and the due date, and put it in a folder with their name on it.

 ## Magic Question #5

"Who can do this task besides me?"

The more you delegate appropriately, the less you will have to struggle—and isn't that the goal? I expect you'll be making a lot of Name Folders now, right?

Keep your Name Folders with your Control Folders where you can access them easily.

At this point, all my Cross-Dominant ✈ clients sigh and tell me, "Well, I'll delegate the fun stuff and keep all the hard work for myself."

Why? You're paying people, aren't you? If they get to do all the fun stuff, why aren't *they* paying *you*?

HOW TO MAKE SURE THE TASK YOU'RE DELEGATING GETS DONE

People often ask me how to make sure the tasks they are delegating will get done. Once they're off your desk, they're easy to forget, so try this: Get a phone message book (with self-carbons) and use it for instructions.

From now on, when you delegate a task, write it in the book with the delegatee's name, the date it was assigned, and the date it's due. Use as many phone message slips as you need for each task.

Tear the white copy off and give it to them. Keep the yellow copy in the message book and put it in your desk drawer.

When they come back and ask a question about the task, when they return the completed task, or if they claim you never assigned it to them, open the drawer, take out the book, and refer to your original note . . .

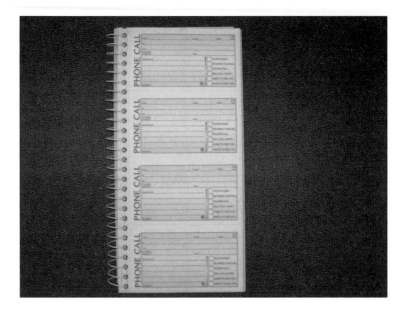

This method gives you a chance to remind them of the task, and later to compare the due date with the date they actually completed it. It also lets them know you're keeping track of everything you ask them to do.

Some people ask me, "Why not just send them an e-mail?" Answer: they already have too many e-mails to sort through, print out, collate and keep track of. This is low-tech enough to have a big impact. Besides, e-mails can be missed, remain undelivered, or get "lost" (and I say that in air quotes).

You might have to hire more help, but did you know creating jobs is an excellent way to make more money? Figure out your own hourly worth, then pay someone a lower rate to do the smaller dollar jobs. Let's say you could be earning $15 per hour, but you lose time when you stop to do your filing—so pay someone else $7.50 per hour to do it, and get ahead of the game.

Maybe you already have enough help. Are you using it? The more you ask yourself the "who else" Magic Question, the more you are training yourself to delegate.

If you're not used to delegating, remember that no one is born knowing how. It's something we learn.

✤ How Henry Ford Delegated the Model T

Ford invited the press to watch his new Model-Ts roll off the assembly line. Everyone was astounded! One journalist asked, "How does the internal combustion engine work?" Ford said, "I don't know." The journalist looked puzzled. "Well," asked another journalist, "how do you make the body parts so uniformly?" "I don't know," said Ford. This went on until one frustrated journalist exclaimed, "You're Henry Ford! Why don't you know how these things are made?" Said Ford calmly, "I don't have to know. I just have to hire the people who *do* know."

137

Now back to your stacks of paper: all of a sudden your next step becomes clear, doesn't it? Delegate as much as you can.

◁ If You Have No One to Whom You Can Delegate

1. Decide how much you would pay for help. Would you pay $50 an hour to have that filing done? $30? $15? A total of $100?

   I heard that! Stop saying, "But I can do it myself for nothing." The point isn't whether you *can*. The point is whether you *have*. If you *haven't*, you probably *won't*—unless you get some help.

2. Make a short list of which tasks you want done and how you would expect a helper to behave (for example, "Work cheerfully and be prompt.") List everything you can think of: whether a car and license are necessary, how many words a minute you want typed, everything. Include the hourly rate of pay, how many hours a week you'll need help, and whether you'll want the helper weekdays or weekends, nights or days, and anything else you can think of that's relevant.

3. Now pick up the phone and call your local high school or college. (Don't hire an organizer to file—it's too expensive and it's not a skill match. Organizers are for system changes. Do you really want to pay top dollar for filing?) Ask the school for their job bulletin board or placement department. When you reach that department, tell them you want to fax (or send) them a job description for posting.

4. They will fax or send resumes back to you. Give the applicants chapter one of this book to read, and ask them to identify themselves. You're looking for an Access Type that matches your own.

5. When you find a good helper, schedule several working dates with them. Limit your time to two or three hours per session (less time means you won't get enough done to make it worth your while, and more time will leave you so wiped out you won't try it again.)

If you don't like any of those suggestions, here are a few alternatives:

- find some way to reduce your workload

- change jobs

- clone yourself

- hire your teenager or someone else's

- trade tasks with someone in your office

Warning: Do *not* use your partner or spouse as your part-time helper. Your style and access will be compromised, and emotions will arise that may take quite a bit of untangling.

▷ How to Get Tasks to Your Helper

Let's say you decide to delegate a task to Mortimer. How will you make sure that Mortimer gets it? Your urgent e-mail is going to look just like dozens of other e-mails, and you can't send any hard-copy maps, charts, binders or documentation that way.

Do you want to drop everything and get the paperwork to him now? No? Good! Right answer! Remember, don't interrupt yourself unless it's an emergency.

Instead, try this: Ask yourself, When do I see Mortimer?

Magic Question #6

🕐,👁 "When will I see the person?

✋,👁 "Where will I be when I see them?"

Examples:

- Monday Staff Meeting

- Carpool

- Your Own Office

- Trade Show

- Their Office

- Special Event

Let's say you see Mortimer every Monday at the Staff Meeting.

Now ask yourself, What do I always have with me at the Monday Staff Meeting? Let's assume you always have your briefcase.

Magic Question #7

"What else will I have with me when I need this?"

- Briefcase

- Box

- Palm Pilot

- Folder

Now make a Control Folder (close your eyes and check the color first) and label it, "Take to Monday Staff Meeting" (or your best choice along those lines).

Ha! You thought I was going to tell you to make a folder labeled "Mortimer," didn't you? You could do that, but how would that motivate you to take the folder to the Monday Staff Meeting? Remember to Backwards Up from your goal, and label the folder with your *first* step.

Add a stickie that stands up so it will be sure to catch your eye while you're in front of Mortimer. Then put the briefcase near the door, in the car, or somewhere else you cannot possibly miss it. When you get to the Monday Staff Meeting, open the briefcase and there is your stickie, sticking up, catching your eye, and reminding you what to do!

▷ **More Delegation Tips**

- Put up a sign on your desk that says, "Who can do this task besides me?"

- You *can* afford help. Start by hiring someone three hours a week—you can handle that. (Getting used to having help may take some time if you've been depriving yourself, but you can turn things around, a few hours at a time.)

- Be clear and fair. Tell the person what you expect and when you need it. Better still, write it down.

- Use Name Folders to help you delegate more and forget less. Make a folder with each victim's—uh, I mean delegatee's—name on it, and start channeling more and more tasks over to them. (Remember, people are *very* curious about what's inside a folder with their name on it.)

- If you're not getting all your paperwork done at night, take home less paperwork.

ABOUT PDA'S (PERSONAL DIGITAL ASSISTANTS) OR ELECTRONIC HAND-HELD DEVICES

🕐 CHRONS: If you're a Chron you love your PDA. You are probably saying, "What's all this blather about verbing paper? Why doesn't everyone just put everything in a Palm Pilot? Why bother with date stickies or calendars?" The answer is this: Each Access Type retrieves things differently. Not everyone works well with a PDA.

Besides, your upcoming event might have a map, directions, long text or other backup that just isn't worth scanning or inputting to your PDA. Never mind—I knew I wouldn't be able to talk you Chrons🕐 out of your beloved PDAs!

👁 VISUALS: Those electronic organizer screens are just too small for you! Laptops are better: They hold more stuff than a PDA, they can be networked, they can make calls and access the internet. Other advantages of laptops include the larger screen, improved graphics capabilities, and now the ability to burn CDs.

✋ SPATIALS: You will not do well with a PDA because you prefer the feel of paper. You also like your paper calendar because the size of each little date box shows you how much time you have in the day. You dislike peering at little screens, too. You might use your PDA to hook up to your computer and print out a calendar, but you still prefer to end up with paper. If you are a Spatial ✋ and you have been considering buying a PDA, you may want to reconsider.

✈ CROSS-DOMINANTS: You have way too much stuff to fit into a PDA. Your "stuff" can include blueprints, huge financial reports, manuals, petri dishes, tile samples, food, videotapes, bicycle tires, and more. It's impossible to input all that. An even bigger problem, though, is your lack of input time.

Solution: use whatever calendar or contact database you like best. Don't force yourself to use a PDA, and don't let anyone talk you into one unless you love it (in which case you probably are a Chron 🕘).

Chapter 11
How to Relieve the Tyranny of To-Do Lists

> *How does your To-Do list work with all this?*
> *How can you turn your To-Dos into*
> *To-Dones faster and more efficiently?*

◁ I Just Got Organized and My In-Bin is Full Again!

Does it feel like a tsunami of paper is crashing over you? Of course there will always be more To-Dos comin' atcha, but here's a tip to disarm them: There are three kinds of To-Dos. Keep them separate.

1. Un-verbed: these are To-Dos you haven't looked at or reviewed yet. They're still in your In-Bin, or you can put them back there if you haven't had time to verb them yet.

2. Verbed but not yet in Control Folders: these are things that must wait for more input or decisions before going into a Control Folder. Put them back into the In-Bin to marinate. You'll be able to spot them easily because of the verbs you wrote on them.

3.   Foldered: these To-Dos are verbed, in
     their Control Folders, and ready for you
     to work on whenever you want to and
     not a minute sooner. (Well, OK, when you
     have to, but we can dream, can't we?)

◁   The Cure for, "What Did I Come in Here For?"

Now hold on to your hat, because here's a radical thought: Your brain is full.

Mental space is increasingly precious. We are constantly bombarded with messages, information, and demands. Traditional organizing books have all borrowed from the first, classic time management books that were written long before the internet and e-mail were invented. That old information simply does not apply any longer.

You can't work smoothly when your brain is full. If you try to hang onto all your thoughts at one time, mentally keeping them in priority order and acting upon them in logical turn, one more request can send you over the edge. Have you ever snapped at some poor innocent just because they asked a simple question when you were trying to hold your brains in with both hands so all your To-Dos wouldn't leak out your ears?

Now imagine adding just one more To-Do: instant meltdown. If your brain were a computer, the screen would say, "crash—please restart."

If you keep having the experience of walking into a room and forgetting what you went in there for, your brain is full.

What happens when you try to cram too many books on a shelf? Some fall off because gravity always prevails. It's the same with the To-Dos you're keeping in your mind: The more you try to hold onto, the more you lose. You may *not* have a memory problem: You may just be trying to fit twenty pounds of To-Dos into a ten-pound brain.

Stop trying to remember things. Don't even let them into your memory in the first place. If you never take them in they won't be able to weigh on you. You will be able to deal with interruptions easily when they come up. Crises won't kill you, you'll be less brittle, more peaceful, and you may even be able to start cutting down on caffeine.

❖ A Genius and His Memory: Einstein

Albert Einstein once went to dinner with a friend and a new acquaintance. Over dinner, the new acquaintance asked Einstein for his phone number. "Sure," said Al. He got up, left the table, and walked back toward the phones. "Where is he going?" asked the acquaintance. "I don't know," said the friend, with a puzzled look on his face …

Einstein came back and handed the man a slip of paper with his phone number on it. "My God, you're Einstein!" said the guy. "Why do you have to look up your own phone number?" Einstein said, "Why should I keep in my mind the little things I can find anywhere?"

▷ How to Stop Carrying the Little Things

Think about how much stress you'd avoid if you could refrain from holding all your To-Dos in your mind at once. What if you could think about only what you need for this moment, and never be afraid of losing the rest? Here's how.

◁ How to Do the Core Memory Dump

Whenever you think of something you have to do, grab that 3" x 5" notepad you bought on your supply run, or pick up an index card or any old scrap of recycled paper, and write it down.

Always start writing *in the middle* of the page. Why the middle? Because you'll almost always think of something you have to do *before that*. Move up.

If you start writing traditionally at the top and then remember other things you need to do *before that*, you'll have to squeeze in tiny writing that makes your lists look crazy and intimidates you into "accidentally" losing them. In other words, you'll have no room left to Backwards Up.

Be smart. Start in the middle, and give yourself the luxury of working either up or down.

As you finish writing each new To-Do (one task to a page, please), put it into a verbed Control Folder (if you know the verb), or toss it into your In-Bin (if it needs to marinate longer). Or you can put a stack of To-Dos in your pocket, go run errands, and throw them out as you go.

At the end of the day if you have any leftover To-Do Notes, simply put them back on your desk, in your In-Bin, in your Control Folders, or in your calendar. Put them wherever they will motivate you to get them done when the time is ripe.

MANY PEOPLE TELL ME, "I DON'T NEED TO WRITE THAT DOWN, I'LL REMEMBER IT."

Sure you will. Or not. But why bother entering it into your memory when you can skip that step and jot it down now? You might as well; you've got it in front of you.

Putting To-Dos into your memory means you will have to work to remember them later, which means you will be interrupting yourself again at that time—but when that time comes, you may be busy, and will probably not appreciate the self-interruption. Do yourself a favor and write them down now.

▷ A Cool To-Do Trick

Remember, we are dealing with real life here, not some perfectly sanitized situation frozen in time. Because you work, because you have projects, and because all your projects have multiple steps, you *will* have paper on your desk. The next tip shows you how to use color as a kind of shorthand to regain control. Just don't use too many colors, or you'll waste a lot of time remembering which color goes with which verb (or you could write them down—naw, that'd be too easy!).

AN EXCELLENT WAY TO COLOR-CODE YOUR TO-DOS (OPTIONAL)

- Buy colored paper
- Cut it into quarter-sized notes and keep them within reach

- Think about your verbs. What do you do in a day? Delegate, input, run errands, etc. Assign a color to each verb. My "Delegate" notes are blue, my "Input to computer" notes are orange, and my "Run errands" notes are pink, etc. Consult your Inner Organizer, then choose appropriate colors!
- When you think of a To-Do, grab the appropriate color and jot a To-Do Note.

Later, if you want to, you can group all your notes by verb. This is especially helpful if you have to carry your To-Dos from one location to another.

When I'm rushing out the door to run errands I grab just the pink "Errand" To-Dos. When I'm looking for a computer-related note on my desk, I look at only the orange notes. Use colors to make it easy to find—and finish—your To-Dos!

Note: If you hate this idea, don't do it!

A NOTE TO PDA FANS:

Linears ✔ and Chrons ⊕, once again, you are probably impatient with all of the above, thinking how much easier it is to use your Palm Pilot or Visor. Remember though, our friends the Spatials 🖐 and the Visuals 👁 need the feel of paper moving through their hands as a tangible or visible reminder of what they have to do.

▷ The Last Time You'll Ever Have to Rewrite a To-Do List

Please take five minutes, *right now*, and make To-Do Notes for all the tasks you can think of. Go as far into the future as you can. Your objective is to empty out your mind. If you have already written your To-Dos on a list somewhere, please rewrite them now as new To-Do Notes. This will be the last time you'll ever have to rewrite your To-Dos!

Write one note for each task you have to do. If you are going to the store to buy five items, that's one task. (You don't need five notes unless you plan to go to the store five times.) Put the verb in the upper right-hand corner of the note: Will you shop? Go to the store? Run an errand? The choice is yours. Which verb or phrase will motivate you to complete the task?

155

Some people ask me if they should write a note to remind them to check their e-mail and the hundreds of other things they do daily. If you might forget the task, write it down. If you do it automatically, you don't have to write it down.

IF YOU HATE TO-DO NOTES, DON'T USE 'EM!

If you love your To-Do list and it works for you, keep it and don't switch to To-Do Notes. (But I wonder; if it works so well, why are you reading a book on how to get organized?)

 ## Magic Question #8

"Might I forget to do this task?"

If so, write a note. If not, you don't need a note.

▷ How to Deal with New To-Dos

After you have transferred your To-Dos onto notes, go over them one more time and make sure there's a verb on each one. Make the verb easy to see by putting a box or circle around it.

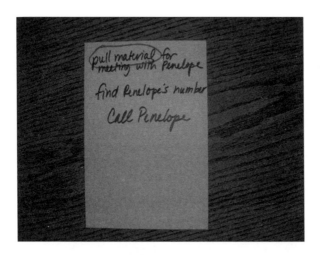

Remember, the purpose of the circled verb is to prevent you from reading the note over and over, trying to remember what you meant when you wrote the To-Do. It will also motivate you to complete the task.

Do you have my permission to write out your To-Dos and put them directly into your Control Folders without putting verbs on them? Sure, why not? But if you drop the folders you'll have to start over from scratch.

THE ADVANTAGES OF USING TO-DO NOTES INSTEAD OF ONE ALL-ENCOMPASSING TO-DO LIST

- To-Do lists have to be rewritten daily. To-Do Notes never need to be rewritten.

- Every time you add an item to your To-Do list, it feels like another chore. If you write it on a To-Do Note, you will be rid of it soon. (One note can be finished and tossed, but a list is never done. Which would you rather have?)

- To-Do lists must be carried around with you, which creates one more burden. With To-Do Notes, you can take along just the ones you need.

- To-Do lists can't be re-prioritized. To-Do Notes can be shuffled into priority order easily. If a lower priority item suddenly becomes higher priority, just shuffle that note to the top of the stack.

- To-Do Notes can be sorted any way you want: by verb (so you can make all your calls at once), by date (to see everything due at once) or even by color. When they're completed, they can go into a file (as a record of what you did), or they can serve as a reminder for next time. To-Do lists can't be sorted at all.

- Hey, all you Spatials 🖐! Do you want to feel more progress as you work through your To-Do Notes? Save them to show how much you've gotten done! Toss your completed To-Dos into a basket near your desk. When you feel depressed, haul the basket out and look at it. Wow! Look how much you've *done!*

▷ Avoiding a Typical Organizing Trap

Get used to separating your work into two phases:

1. Prepping it: getting your work set up and ready to do, versus

2. Actually doing the work

Combining these two steps is a trap. Keeping them separate will save your sanity.

It *seems* to take longer to write out the notes than to do the tasks on them, but it doesn't really. As soon as you try using To-Do Notes, you'll realize how much time you've been wasting, chasing down each task and wrestling it to the ground the very second you think of it.

To-Do Notes take far less time because you no longer let your mind jerk you from one To-Do to another, so you have time to finish far more of them. Time is lost not when you're working, but when you're changing tracks, losing your place, and then having to figure out where you left off so you can get back on track.

Stay on track. When you think of something you have to do, jot a quick To-Do Note, set it aside, and get back to what you were doing. This will keep you from sparkling all over the place.

ABOUT STAYING IN ONE MODE

I just looked at my e-mail and I see that it's time to send in my check for a business women's luncheon that takes place next month.

As tempting as it is to whip out the check-book and get the payment in the mail right now while it's on my mind, I know that doing so will divert me from writing this book. Since I've planned to be "in the writing mode" this afternoon, if I interrupt myself now, I will complain tomorrow that I didn't get much writing done.

Instead, I'll take a few seconds now to jot a To-Do Note reminding me to send the check. I can do that much without leaving my writing mode. Both this book *and* the check will get written, and the check will be mailed in plenty of time. You *can* have it both ways when you later your To-Dos and stay in one mode.

▷ Latering Again

Practice saying this out loud: "Some of this is not going to get done. Which of these things can wait?" Then put *reasonable* To-Do dates on them.

Magic Question #9

"Which of these things can wait?"

Something's gotta give! You *cannot* get everything in the whole world done in the time you have allotted. Sorry, it's true! Don't kill me; I'm just the messenger.

Here's Another Traditional Organizing Rule That Just Flames Me

"Put your To-Dos in priority order and code them with an A, B, or C to designate when they should be done."

You don't need codes. Codes will cause more problems than they solve, because you have to remember what they mean, or look them up, or translate them. Why not use dates and times? Now *there's* a system we already have in place—and it works!

Chapter 12
How to Simplify Projects

> *Why does some paperwork take so much longer than other paperwork? Why does work keep expanding, or does it just seem that way? What's the best way to corral all the related items when they won't fit into a regular file?*

◁ **How Some Paperwork Has Been Fooling You**

Projects are not the same as To-Dos. To-Dos can be completed relatively quickly. All the To-Dos we've talked about so far are what I call "one-shot" tasks: "Make a call," "Send a fax," or "Type an e-mail," and you're done.

Projects take longer because they have lots of steps and often the steps are of varying sizes. Projects can include huge, medium, and tiny tasks, repetitious tasks, and even bits of other tasks already in progress.

If it meets *any* of the following criteria, it's a project:

- It has more than one step (requiring multiple verbs)

- It has more than one due date

- It has all different kinds of detail tasks under one large heading (e.g., "Meeting" or "Newsletter")

HOW PROJECTS ARE DIFFERENT

Project Title:	Actual Project:
Set up meeting	Set up meeting, hire caterer, find and interview speaker, research venue, book hotel rooms, negotiate for transportation
Write newsletter	Write and produce newsletter, develop mailing list, design layout, import graphics, select print vendor, track subscribers, update database

Have you been thinking of your projects as one-shot tasks? If so, you're not alone. Again, one of the major causes of disorganization is underestimating the time a task will take. Once you realize which items are projects, you can plan your time more effectively.

▷ How Multiple To-Dos Sneak Up on You

Some projects are relatively small and can fool you. Let's say you've received an e-mail from a prospective client and it asks you for three things. Using a traditional organizing To-Do list, you would jot one item ("Answer e-mail from client"). From now on, write all three of the actions you need to take. Let's say they are,

- Send a catalogue

- E-mail an article

- Add the client to your mailing list

Don't be misled into thinking that your response will take "just a few minutes." This is a project because it requires multiple actions. In this case there are three actions, so it will take at least three times as long as you had originally estimated to finish this particular To-Do.

Small projects like this can circulate through your Control Folders in the order in which they need to occur. There are two ways to do this:

1. Print out the e-mail and use it instead of a To-Do Note. Write a verb next to each of the three requests (send, e-mail, add to mailing list). Then put this printout into the first Control Folder ("Send"), until you have time to send the catalogue.

   As soon as that's done, cross off the verb *send* and move the printout into the second Control Folder ("E-mail"). When that's done, cross off *e-mail* and put the printout in the third Control Folder ("Add to mailing list").

In this fashion, the note or printout moves from folder to folder so you neither have to search for it, nor keep it out on your desk between steps.

2. Print out three hard copies. (Stop gasping! Paper is cheaper than brain cells.) Put one in each pertinent Control Folder ("Send," "E-mail," "Add to mailing list"). Handle each task as you have time.

How do you know which method to use? Whichever one motivates you to get the task done.

Just remember: any time there are multiple steps, you're looking at a project. That means both the time and the chances for interruptions and mistakes increase.

▷ Why It's OK if Your Desk is Full

Whenever I see stacks of paper on someone's desk, I know I'm looking at projects. Projects are usually tall, vertical stacks of paper as opposed to papers spread out low and horizontally. Take a look at your own desk: Do you see any tall stacks? They're projects, aren't they?

Why are those projects out on your desk, instead of being put away, as traditional organizing books recommend? It's simple: because you're working on them. Not only is it illogical to put them away and take them out again dozens of times a day, it would also cause you to lose papers, misplace folders, and forget parts of your projects. Projects are one of the main reasons we don't clear off our desks before we go home at night.

Projects can include books, directories, videotapes, CDs, binders, manuals, color charts, blueprints, and much, much more. It doesn't make sense to keep them in Control Folders—they're just too bulky.

We need some way to deal with projects as the special category they really are, and some place to store them that is neither on the desk nor hidden away in the drawers.

◁ Where to Keep Bulky Projects

Let's say you have agreed to take on a new project. Where can you keep all the bits and pieces so you can dip into it when you need to, without disrupting your other work? The answer starts with knowing the size of the project.

▷ How to Store Smallish Projects

If your paperwork for the new project is relatively slim at this point. . .

1. Choose a colored folder. (Synesthetes 👂 decide on the color with your eyes closed.)

2. Label it with a noun (example: "Newsletter").

Remember: this Project Folder is temporary. It will soon fill to overflowing, but for now it's just a convenient place to start gathering the paperwork, objects and ideas that will kick off this project.

Now that you've made the folder, you're probably thinking, How am I going to keep all the parts of this project straight? There are several ways:

A. Plan and track the steps of your project by using the *outside* of the folder as a checklist. Write all the steps of the project

(Backwardsing Up, starting at the bottom) on the front of the folder. Write the due date next to each step. As you finish each step, check it off, and add your initials and the date you completed it. (This works especially well when several people are involved in one project.)

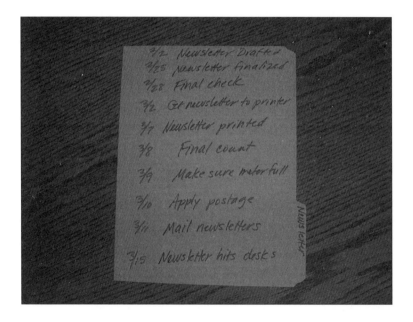

Or. . .

B. Use the *inside* of the folder to plan and track your progress on the project. Using stickies, show the "stepping stones" to completion.

Ask yourself, What steps must be taken? Be sure that each stickie equals just one step, so you can throw away the stickie when the step is finished.

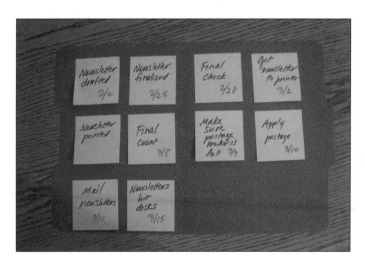

With this stickie method, if you get the steps out of order you can rearrange them easily.

As your project grows, you can add more folders in the same color, or you can expand it into bins as explained in the next section.

▷ How to Store Largish Projects

For storing your larger projects, I *totally* recommend what I call "Bins-On-a-Shelf." When you use bins on shelves, you can reach them to bring entire projects down to your desk, work on them, reach up again to put them away, and clear your desk quickly when you need to look good fast.

The bins have another advantage: You can toss things in easily without having to arrange them over and over, and when you're ready to work on a project all your stuff is together.

A good example of a project that could have its own bin is the much-beloved balancing of the checkbook. If you have filled up a check register, toss it in the bin. If you have a deposit confirmation or an ATM receipt, toss it in the bin. If you need to look something up in an old register and it's not urgent, toss it in the bin. You may be receiving cancelled checks from the bank—guess what? Into the bin they go.

At the end of the month (or whenever you get around to balancing the checkbook and reconciling the statement) all the parts and pieces will be together. This "bin" method also makes it very easy to delegate the entire check-balancing project to a bookkeeper, partner or otherwise willing victim—um, I mean, helper.

A TRICK FOR BALANCING YOUR CHECKBOOK

Here's a trick for balancing a checkbook that hasn't been balanced in—well, let's say forever.

Go to your bank and open a second checking account. Find out the balance on your first account. Move most of the money from your first account to the new, second account. If you're afraid some checks will bounce, move less money.

Use the new checking account for several months. At the end of that time, ask your bank for the balance on both accounts. Assume they are correct. Move most of the remaining money from the second account back to the first account. Use the first account for the next several months.

In other words, let the bank balance your account for you. They do it anyway, don't they? And you're paying for it anyway, aren't you?

It's not perfect, but it's a heck of an improvement over never having the account balanced at all.

Oh, stop gasping. Before reading this book, you were stuck between perfection and never getting anything done. Now you've been introduced to "Good Enough Organizing," and you know what? It gives you one less thing to think about.

You'll be much more willing to complete your projects if each has its own bin and is kept separate from the others. Make sure the project bins you use most often are closest to you.

Also, make sure the papers, books and other parts of your projects don't sneak out of the bins to lie directly on the shelves. If they're loose, they'll spread all over the place—you know they will!—and you will end up with the same mess you had before, only worse.

When you run out of space on flat surfaces, always go up, up, up the walls! If you can't put shelves on the walls, place a bookcase behind you or beside you as one part of your U-shaped desk configuration.

Projects don't need to stay on your desk all the time, but when you need them they must be consolidated and easy to reach—and bookcases are one of the cheapest and easiest ways to do this.

Chapter 13
How to Maximize Findability

> *How many times have you had to stop working to find something? Is there a better way to place things so you'll always find them easily?*

◁ Why "A Place For Everything" Doesn't Always Work

A lot of traditional organizing books tell you to, "Find a place for everything and keep it there". That works only for Spatials 🖐—and then only part of the time. Here's a better idea: Ask yourself where you're going to look for them.

As you encounter each item, repeat this question. Then make a label with your answer on it, and paste it to the box, Control Folder, bin, or whatever container you're using.

This changes your noun (what is the item?) to a *circumstance*, and that circumstance is the best possible thing to put on your label. Next time you look at that label you'll trust it because *you* wrote it based on *your* best advice at the time *you* were preparing for *your* future use of that material.

 # Magic Question #10

👁 *"Under what circumstances will I want to see this again?*

✋ *"Where will I use this next time?"*

🕐 *"When will I want to use this again?"*

EXAMPLES OF ANSWERS:

If your answer is the one on the left, make the label shown on the right.

• Holiday decorations . . .

>Open November 30th

• 5 year old tax stuff . . .

>If I Am Audited

• Expense reports . . .

>Compare to Reimbursements

• Motivational sayings. . . .

>When I'm Feeling Low

The same concept works for files and filing, which we'll cover in depth in chapter 15.

Here's Another Traditional Organizing Rule That Just Flames Me

"Have a place for everything and keep it in its place."

I prefer Mark Twain's version: "A place for everything, and keep it somewhere else. This is not advice, this is merely custom."

◁ How to Find Things

If you have trouble finding things that you *know* you've handled, ask yourself Magic Question #11.

Magic Question #11

"What was the action I was going to take?"

- If the answer is "Call," look in the call folder

- If the answer is "Fax," look in the fax folder

- If the answer is, "Listen to it in the car," look in the car and there it will be, because *you* set it up according to how *you* wanted to access it.

▷ **Only *You* Get to Decide Where You Want Things**

Once your office is organized you will be able to find anything easily. How will you *ever* become that organized? By **placing** things with your eyes closed. This removes your preconceived notion of where things "should" go, and teaches you to rely on your Inner Organizer. When you use this exercise, you stop looking for things and go right to finding them.

➡ Here's How to Place Things Where You'll Find Them

- Pick up your stapler

- Close your eyes

- Now, without looking, place it wherever you're going to want it

Voila! That's how you decide where things go from now on. The more you practice placing things with your eyes closed, the more you will be able to find things without looking—and you'll find them every time. This is true for all Access Types. Stop asking, "Now where did I put that?" You can eliminate many self-interruptions every day by using this placing technique.

Now do the same placing exercise with your phone, calculator, tape, paper clips, pens, Control Folders, etc.—all the stuff that you used to spend so much time looking for. Place them where you're going to want them, and when you want them, there they'll be.

Magic Question #12

"Where am I going to want it?"

"Where will I be sitting when I use it?"

Will you want it beside you? Behind you? On a shelf?

Will you be sitting in your office chair? In your car? At your desk?

❖ Three Ways to Set Things Up So You Can Access Them Easily

1. Catherine's Coffee Cup

One of the first organizing projects I did was in 1979 for a journalist named Catherine. Her editor had told her to submit to an organizing session with me. Sacrificing everything for the cause, she allowed me to reorganize her desk and office.

The more we worked together, the more fun we had. As we were finishing she tossed me one last challenge: "Where do I keep my coffee cup? When I'm really busy, my desk gets so full of papers that I sometimes lose it!"

I had her pick up the cup, close her eyes, and place it exactly where she'd like to reach for it. She did, and we memorialized the spot with a small pedestal. Catherine never lost her coffee cup again.

2. Frieda's Audio Tapes

Once I organized the office of a hypnotherapist who had a lot of audio tapes. While we worked, she kept moving them from place to place.

Finally it bothered her enough to ask, "Where should I keep my tapes?" I answered her with this question: "Where do you sit when you listen to them?" Her answer: "In my car." She looked up suddenly and broke into a big smile: "In my car!" she said. "That's where I'll keep my tapes!"

3. Beverly's Books

I recently worked with an Image Consultant who had a beautifully decorated office. As you might imagine, she was very interested in color. When I tested her, she showed Visual 👁 access preferences and was clearly a Cross-Dominant ✈.

We talked about her bookcase. She wanted to keep all her books, but someone had told her to throw out most of them, and arrange the rest by subject. But she didn't want to throw any of them away.

I asked her how she accessed her books, and had her demonstrate rather than just telling me. Of course, she turned around and looked at them (as a Visual 👁 would) rather than reaching for them without looking (as a Spatial 🖐 would).

I suggested that she keep every single one and arrange them all by color. Her whole face lit up. She smiled and said very strongly, "Now *that* will work! I always know the color of the book I want, and that's how I look for it!" In other words, she saw the book's color *in her mind's eye* before she ever turned toward her bookcase.

Your preferences must be recognized as the most important part of your organizing project, or you will end up taking ten steps for every one you mean to take.

If you go home with a backache or neckache every night, ask yourself how much time you spent reaching for things that were not where you first tried to find them. Instead of deciding where they *should* go, figure out where you *want to* find them, and keep them there.

Chapter 14
How to Stay Organized Without Resorting to Discipline

OK! You understand your Organizing Style, Work Personality, and Access Type. You've verbed your papers, flowed your furniture, dated your priorities, and binned and shelved your projects. Now let's put it all together.

◁ How Not to Lose Your Stuff

Remember your Central Headquarters stuff? If it's still in the box, this is the time to bring it back in and unpack it. Let's start with your tools: stapler, tape, scissors, calendar, pencil jar, etc.

Remember placing things with your eyes closed so you'd find them later? This is the time to place the tools from your Central Headquarters box if you haven't done so already.

Here's Another Traditional Organizing Rule That Just Flames Me

"Group similar items."

Naw. Just keep things wherever you'll want to find them, as long as it's convenient. Organize by access, not by category.

Obvious example:

I like to keep pens and notepads all over the place so I don't have to go looking for them. If I kept them all in one place, whenever I wanted to write something down I would have to get up and go there, which means I would be wearing holes in the carpet from trekking back and forth. I'm better off keeping them *everywhere* I'll reach for them. This kind of organizing has more to do with convenience than anything else.

Less obvious example:

It's OK to split up your files. Traditional organizing books tell you to keep all of a category together, but it's better to keep files you access frequently close to you, and files you access less frequently farther away from you. This way you don't have to get up and cross the room every time you need to file frequently-used items. (Sound familiar?)

▷ **How to Keep from Running Around**

Have you set up your Holding Tanks for papers to be filed, read, input, and so on? Are the Tanks big enough? Are they close enough to toss stuff into easily, and far enough to keep from obstructing the flow? Good! It'll save you a lot of running around.

◁ **What Mode Are You In?**

Sort when you are in a sorting mode and work when you are in a working mode. If you find yourself trying to do both at once, it means there's something else on your mind. If this is the case, make a conscious decision to leave the sorting mode. Put all your un-verbed papers back in the In-Bin, switch to the working mode, and handle whatever was bothering you. Then switch back later and finish sorting and verbing.

▷ **How to Keep from Getting Stuck Again**

Make sure your Control Folders (in their Folder Holder) are nearby so you can see them *and* reach them without standing up, squinting, reaching, leaning, or knocking things over. Don't put them in a drawer. "Out of sight, out of mind" applies to all Access Types.

When you're ready, hit it again: Pull papers one at a time from your In-Bin, attach stickies with verbs and dates, and get them into your Control Folders.

If you're reluctant to take things *out* of your In-Bin to sort them, it's because the In-Bin is too deep for you to see into, or it's so big that it holds an intimidating amount of paper. Try this: Take just one handful of papers at a time from the In-Bin. Sort and verb them, then get them into your Control Folders. Take a quick break for a glass of water or a walk around the block, then take another handful, and so on. When you have time, get a shallower In-Bin—one you can see into (look for a mesh or translucent bin).

➡ Here's How to Use Your Control Folders

1. Each day, review your Control Folder labels. (You don't have to look at the *contents* of every file every day, just the *labels*—yay! That alone will cut your work time substantially.) Determine which folders you want to work with, pull them out, and put them on top of your desk. (If the labels don't motivate you to *want* to pull them out, consider revising the labels.)

2. Stand up! This makes it easier to see an "overview" of your desk. (This is especially important for Cross-Dominants ➤ and Spatials ✋.)

3. Let's say you've decided to start with calls. Open the "Call" folder and prioritize your call

To-Do Notes by laying them out like a deck of cards. Put the most urgent on the left, medium priority in the middle, and the least important on the right.

Now put them back together in priority order with the most urgent on top, and put the whole stack back in the "Call" folder.

You couldn't do this with a list, could you? Now you see the advantage of writing To-Do Notes instead of a To-Do list: You can juggle and shuffle To-Dos as your priorities change.

4. Now make your first call—the one on top of the stack. If they're not in and you must leave a message, jot the word "message" on the call slip, along with the date. This prevents you from calling again too soon, or waiting too long to try them back.

   Clip your "message" note to the inside left of your "Call" folder. This now becomes your "Waiting for a callback" section. When you receive a callback from one you made earlier, open the "Call" folder and look on the inside left. There are your notes, reminding you of what you wanted to talk about.

5. Continue with your other calls. As you finish each one, decide if there is any other action to be taken. If there is, put the To-Do Note or phone message slip into the appropriate Control Folder (be sure to note dated items

on your calendar.) If there's nothing more to do, throw it away, or put it in your "Input to address database" Control Folder or your "To be filed" Holding Tank. When you are finished making calls, close the "Call" folder and put it back in the Folder Holder.

6. If you are interrupted but not yet ready to put the "Call" folder away, use a colored piece of paper to show where you left off. Deal with the interruption, then open the "Call" folder again, find your place, and continue making calls.

7. If you have time, choose another folder and follow the same process.

8. When you are done for the day, put any newly verbed To-Do Notes into their appropriate Control Folders or Project Bins, and any un-verbed notes back into your In-Bin so you will see them again tomorrow.

ALTERNATE METHOD
(better for Chrons ⏱)

1. Pull the Control Folders you need to work with.

2. Open the first folder and sort the To-Do Notes inside of it by due date.

3. Take out only the To-Do Notes you need to do today. Put the rest of them back in the

folder. Do the same thing with each folder until all the To-Dos for today, regardless of verb, are on your desk in front of you.

4. Stand up for a better overview. Prioritize today's To-Dos into several stacks, putting the most urgent on the left, the "If I Get Around To It Today" in the middle, the "These Could Really Wait" on the right, and the "Oh, #*$%@!!" on the far left.

5. Handle them in the order they're due, from left to right. If you are interrupted, at least the most urgent work is done first, regardless of which verb it carries. Put the rest back in your In-Bin for tomorrow.

◁ How to Keep Your Desk Clear

Whenever you're using your desk and it gets cluttered, take a moment to clear a space in the middle. Put your project bins up on the shelf and put any loose papers back in your In-Bin. You'll feel much more organized when the desktop is clear, especially if you're a Visual 👁 or a Spatial ✋.

Get in the habit of clearing your desk for access, not just for neatness.

190

Chapter 15
How to Get Rid of Filing Fast

How will you ever get around to your filing, much less get to the bottom of it?

Most people hate filing. I think it's because they've already finished working with those papers, and touching them again makes them feel like they've done the job twice.

Here's another reason people hate filing: They feel they've paid their dues and don't need to show no stinkin' badges. Usually they're right. But the filing still sits there, unfiled.

If something needs action, don't file it. Put it in a Control Folder (or back in your In-Bin if it needs to marinate). If it does need filing, consider whether you can let it sit a while longer.

◁ When You Can Procrastinate Filing

While you're still gasping about letting filing sit, consider this: Most filing really can wait, can't it? The important thing is to know which filing is urgent and which is not, and act accordingly.

If you're in a Working Mode, stay with it. Later on, when you're in a Filing Mode, you can file.

▷ How Long Can You Put Off Filing?

Traditional organizing books say that we must file everything as soon as we possibly can. I *really* disagree with this one! Here's a method I like much better.

It's natural to drag your feet if you have to get up too frequently to walk across the room, so separate the "Urgent" from the "Later" filing. Put the "Later" filing into a Holding Tank under your desk or beside it (where you won't bump it with your feet or legs). When it's time to file, pull the "To be filed" Tank out and file away. In the meantime, ignore it.

Sure, *some* filing needs to get filed right away—the papers you want to find in the very near future must be accessible. But why stress over it? The mistake is thinking that all filing has the same urgency. It doesn't.

The trick to getting urgent filing done quickly is to have at least one file drawer very near you. If you already have one near you but it's full, you're going to need at least one more within reach.

Why? You are more likely to file while things are still in your hands *only* if there's space in the drawer, so be sure you have enough space. And even though you are thinking, But I can weed out that drawer, I'm thinking, C'mon, who are you kidding? You haven't done it so far, which means you probably won't do it; but it's not your fault. You've been dealing with much more important matters. Go ahead—give yourself another filing drawer.

Why stress out on April 10th when you can't find all your deductions, if you can slip them into a folder quickly and easily now? The key is keeping the drawer—and the files—nearby and easy to access.

◁ How to Make Filing Easier

You can get your filing out of the way easily by labeling each piece with a **noun** before it leaves your hands. Why a noun? Because it indicates that no action is required. Remember, verbs motivate, but nouns just sit there—like your filing.

Pencil a noun on each piece indicating where (under which topic) you want it filed, then put it in a Holding Tank. This technique offers three advantages:

1. It allows filing to wait a while. These *nouned* papers need no action and convey no urgency.

2. Filing time is reduced because your penciled noun eliminates having to decide and file at the same time. It seems like it would take more time to do these two steps separately, but it doesn't. Remember that *thinking* about where to file and *filing* are two different modes: one is thoughtful and one is brainless— but only if the papers have been appropriately nouned.

3. It's much easier to delegate your filing when you've nouned it, because you know where it will end up. You can do

one task (the nouning), and hire out the other (the dreaded filing).

Watch out! If you delegate your filing without penciling in the noun, you may never see it again. Helpers tend to file things either where *they* want to file them, or they leave things unfiled because they don't know where *you* want them filed. Believe me, it will take just one or two errors before you *love* jotting down that noun.

How do you know which noun to pencil in? Traditional organizing tells you to ask yourself, Where do I want to file this? I've found it works better to ask, Where will I look for this? Listen to your answer— there's your magic noun. Pencil it on the upper right-hand corner of the item to be filed and put the paper in your "To be filed" Holding Tank.

Magic Question #13

"Where will I look for this?"

👁 "Under what word am I going to *look* for this?"

🖐 "Where am I going to *reach* for it?"

🕐 *"When* am I going to want it?"

▷ How to Remove the Pressure to File

I can hear you say, "But won't this mean I'm handling paper twice?" Sure, but who cares? Handling paper twice does not adversely affect the Gross National Product, and besides, it gives you time to think. Remember, to make this trick work you must separate your filing into frequently-accessed files—which get filed right away, and seldom-accessed files—which you can put off.

◁ If You Just Aren't Filing

Remember: If there is a task that you *don't* do, you probably are *unlikely* to do it. You can complain, put yourself down, avoid it, feel guilty, wear a hair shirt, or whatever you want, but you *still* are unlikely to do it. Does filing feel like that to you?

HERE ARE SOME ALTERNATIVES TO AVOIDING FILING

- Get help—whether you pay, trade, or delegate
- Fool yourself into filing one piece at a time while you're on hold or waiting

- Do the urgent filing now, the rest later
- Force yourself to file anyway
- File irregularly *with* guilt
- File irregularly *without* guilt
- Get a personality transplant until you actually *like* filing

---

▷ When Filing <u>Still</u> Isn't Getting Done

There are certain tasks you will never do. It's not that you can't, you just don't. Maybe you don't like them, or they seem trivial, or you're so tired that you never get time, but take heart: There is one more solution.

◁ Getting Help with Your Filing

I figured this out one day when I realized I was doing my helper's work *for* her instead of letting her do it— and it was filing, which I normally hate! It dawned on me that I didn't mind filing at all if there was another person in the room. Now I have a new category for tasks that I prefer to do only when someone else is with me. I call this, "The Companionship Factor."

The Companionship Factor relates to those tasks which you will do *only* if someone is helping you or hanging out with you. It doesn't matter which of you actually *does* the filing; what matters is that you recognize which tasks you *will* do on your own, and which you *won't* do without a companion present. All you need now is to find someone to help you on those tasks.

The tasks for which you want a Companion could be different than anyone else's. For example, some traditional organizing books recommend you have someone with you when you go through your mail, but what if you hate that idea? You might be intensely private, or especially proud of your independence, or insulted by the suggestion that you would need help with something as simple as sorting the mail—but another person may love the suggestion and have entirely different motivations.

Magic Question #14

"Who's the best person to do this task with me?"

If your answer is a name, it's a Companionship Task. If the answer is, "Nobody," it's a task for you to do alone.

Filing and other boring tasks get done sooner, better, and "funner" when someone else is working next to you (especially if you are a Sparklebrain ✹)! Find your own likes and dislikes, and ask for help accordingly.

◁ When Your Helper Doesn't Know Where to File Things

When someone else files for me, anything on which I have not penciled a noun becomes an "I don't know where to file this" item. It's back on my desk because I didn't give the right guidance. My helper gets to put it in a colorful file folder marked, "Tell me where to file these." (Notice she doesn't just mark it, "Where do these go?" because if she doesn't give me an action, I won't open the folder, much less act on it. Know yourself! It saves *so* much time.)

Remember, when you put a piece of paper in the "To be filed" Holding Tank, always pencil a noun at the top indicating *where* it is to be filed (under what word or topic). This way, you've moved it along *two* steps—one with the noun and one by putting it in the Holding Tank. The next time you see it you won't have to start over, asking, "Where was I going to file this?" And it's *so* much easier to delegate filing when you have designated a location with your noun.

▷ Should You Color Code Your Files?

When you put files away *inside* a file drawer, they can be plain manila. They don't need to look fancy, as long as you can find them. Label them any way you want to (any way that's easy to see and to reach). Use neat, simple labels, and *use boring colors* because you don't want them clamoring for your attention.

Or, go ahead! Color code every file in every drawer! It's a lot more expensive, but if a file gets into the wrong drawer you will spot it right away. If you use color-coded files *inside* your drawers, perhaps you'd like each color to stand for a category. What color are financial matters? Legal matters? Close your eyes and choose.

Chapter 16
How to Reduce Interruptions

What really causes interruptions? Can they be controlled? Whose fault are they?

So there you are, working your anatomy off, and the phone rings. You handle the call, eventually disentangle yourself from it and hang up, and somebody bursts into your office. After you've taken care of that, your computer beeps to indicate an incoming e-mail, and then the phone rings again. You haven't even started your paperwork, and you're so fed up you feel like getting drunk and cutting your own hair—and it's only 9:30 in the morning. How will you *ever* get anything done?

Everyone asks me how to prevent interruptions. Aside from eating a steady diet of garlic (which won't stop the phone call or e-mail interruptions), I can't think of anyone, with or without a regular paycheck, who has no interruptions. You'll just have to deal with them, but of course I have some tips for you.

◁ A Trick to Getting Back on Track

Here's a trick: When you are going through paperwork and you get interrupted, put a piece of colored paper or a colored Post-it down to mark your place.

Or, if you're working your way down a list, use a Post-it or colored felt pen to mark where you left off.

If you can't eliminate interruptions completely, at least you can minimize the time it takes to get back on track.

You'll also need to find out if you are the one creating—or allowing—the interruptions.

▷ Who Interrupts You Most Often?

In my experience, most people who suffer frequent interruptions are either allowing them or unwittingly encouraging them. How dare I say that? Let's take a closer look.

Do you . . .

- multitask in a way that shows you are willing to share your attention?

- use one hand to wave to someone to "come on in" while you are talking on the phone, all the while sorting papers with the other hand?

- interrupt yourself in mid-sentence, or let others interrupt you in mid-sentence?

- put one line on hold to talk to someone on another line? Do you use call waiting so frequently that other people are accustomed to interrupting you whenever they want?

- shout through your open doorway or over the top of your cubicle, interrupting other people's work?

- have candy on your desk?

We train people how to treat us, so if you don't want to be interrupted, don't interrupt others, and don't demonstrate that it's OK for others to interrupt you.

I know; now you're going to tell me that it's *other* people doing the interrupting. Think about the bulleted items above for 48 hours and then get back to me.

▷ How to Get People to Leave You Alone So You Can Work

Interruptions do occur, and priorities will always change in midstream, so to some extent you just have to get used to the changes. Still, you can minimize interruptions a couple of ways.

- Stick up for your rights. Tell people what's bothering you.

- Use words that tell people what to do.

    - "My plate's full right now; please come back tomorrow."

    - "I have another obligation. Let's make an appointment for next week."

- "I have just five minutes before I have to leave." (Then stick to it!)

- Everyone's heard this one: Stand up. But here's a twist: Walk out of your own office. The other person has to follow you out, because they are still talking to you, and you're walking away.

- When you've got a long-winded caller on the phone, hang up while *you're* talking. They'll never believe it—they'll think you got disconnected.

◁ How to Explain How Busy You Are

Most people don't realize how busy you are. Some wouldn't care even if they did know, but here are a couple of ways to explain it to everyone else.

- Show them your calendar. Let them see for themselves how busy you are. I like to hand my calendar to people and say, "Take a look and let's see where we can fit you in."

- Behave like an orchestra conductor: Wave one person in, hold up your hand to stop them, wave at another to sit down in the chair. People in our culture are surprisingly obedient and will usually do as you indicate. They won't mind, because they are so strongly trained to take direction. So be a conductor.

WHERE DOES THE TIME GO?

✈ Cross-Dominants are so empathic and nurturing they have a hard time sending people away. They feel responsible for everyone getting everything they need. If you're a Cross-Dominant and you've hired people to do a job, you are doing them—and yourself—a disservice if you do their job for them.

If you're wondering why you never get anything done, maybe it's because you see what people need, stop what you're doing, help them, go back to what you were doing, and—poof! There goes your day. A few days like that and your week is shot, and before you know it—the year.

▷ **Controlling Interruptions**

As you go through each task, practice thinking about what "mode" you are in at the moment.

- Are you in a planning mode?

- Are you in a budget mode?

- Are you in a phone calling mode?

If you are tempted to interrupt yourself, switch to a different task, or start a new project, try this: Say to yourself, I'm still in the calling mode. Then stay in that mode until you've made all the calls you can. This works a lot better than focusing on the negative version, reminding yourself that you haven't finished your calls yet.

Once you learn that controlling interruptions appropriately is a large part of getting organized, you will be able to get back into a regular work rhythm, and you will have fewer and fewer fires to put out.

And take that candy off your desk!

Chapter 17
When You Get the Urge to Purge

What should you toss out, and when should you toss it? Who can keep all their stuff, and who should let theirs go? Learn why the traditional rules are wrong, and review a generic list of stuff to keep versus stuff to toss.

◁ How to Know What Clutter Must Go

Organizing doesn't always mean purging. Purging may not be for you. Getting organized means making things flow efficiently and being able to access them easily. Purging means making things go bye-bye forever. So keep everything you want to keep, as long as you're not hurting anyone.

Here's Another Traditional Organizing Rule That Just Flames Me

"If you haven't used it in six months, throw it out."

That could be your spouse! If you get rid of things before you want to, you'll be sorry later.

▷ When Purging is Painful

New clients often tell me, "I know I have to throw out all my stuff." Some even cry, saying, "I know I need to get organized, but I'm just not ready to get rid of my things yet." They are making the mistake of equating organizing with purging.

When I tell my clients they don't have to get rid of anything unless they want to, I usually get shocked silence in return. They thought they were hiring someone to pry their rigid fingers from their beloved possessions—but I don't do that. I truly believe such "organizing" is harmful. When people aren't ready to let go, forcing them can be so traumatic that the resulting emotional upset is not worth the clean room.

▷ Calling All Hoarders

Hoarders are people who keep way too much stuff for reasons that have nothing to do with the stuff. They can't move through their rooms, they're debilitated by huge mounds of possessions, and they keep bringing in more. Some are even endangering themselves and others physically or psychologically.

If you think you're a hoarder (or share space with one), check with your doctor and ask for a referral to a therapist or support group. Hoarding can be a serious disorder, and is not subject to normal organizing methods—it requires counseling. Nothing less will do. Well-meaning organizers or family members who

207

attempt to get hoarders to part with their stuff can unintentionally do serious emotional damage. Look for someone with a license *and* experience in this matter.

✣ The Collyer Brothers: *Real* Hoarding

In the 1940s two bachelor brothers lived together. They collected newspapers— couldn't bear to part with them. Pretty soon there were stacks of newspapers against the walls, in the middle of the rooms, and eventually the only place left to walk was a narrow path between the papers. It had become a maze.

One day the newspapers collapsed and killed both the brothers.

Now *that's* hoarding!

◁ Not Sure Whether to Let Something Go?

If you can't decide whether to let something go, imagine I come in, take it away from you, and toss it. Would you miss it? Would you get mad at me? If so, keep it! You're not ready to let it go.

Magic Question #15

"If a stranger threw this away, how would I feel about it?"

If you would be sad, mad, or regret it, keep it! Otherwise, out it can go.

Later in this chapter, I propose a list of things to keep and a list of things to toss, but it's only generic advice. As a rule of thumb, I'd rather have you keep things too long than not long enough. You can always throw them out later, but you can't get them back once they're gone.

✤ Sentimental Value vs. Throwing Things Out

A widow called in to one of my radio interviews. Her family had been pressuring her to throw out her dead husband's papers, but every time she tried she was overcome with emotion and couldn't continue. I advised her to keep everything she wanted, for as long as she wanted. She was very relieved by this perspective. She took my advice, and it hurt no one. When she's ready, she'll get rid of them.

Think about your objective: Is it perfection? Rigid discipline, even if it sends someone over the edge? Or is it a *reasonable* degree of order and comfort?

▷ How to Get Someone Else to Throw Their Stuff Away

If someone's "collecting habit" is driving you crazy, you've probably made numerous attempts to get them to throw things out. Hasn't worked, has it?

Try this: At first, don't say anything for a few days (this is to build up your patience and break the nagging cycle you've established). Then, share this book with them and tell them you've realized the error of your ways— you see now that everything they've kept means something special to them.

Next, find a quiet time to ask them the meaning of just one of those things. When they tell you, make a label with their exact words on it, stick it on a large box, and pack their stuff lovingly into the box while they watch.

I'll bet that by the second box, maybe even the first, they'll start saying, "No, that doesn't need to go in there." Soon they'll be throwing things out on their own.

There are three crucial points that make this work.

1.   The label must reflect *exactly* the words they used to describe the meaning of the contents. (I have labeled one box as, "One old shoe and some CD's I couldn't get rid of at a garage sale." Word for word.)

2.   Store the box carefully where it's out of the main area, but where they could get to it if they wanted to. Make sure the label is facing out, or that you have labeled all four sides identically.

3. You must not throw anything out without them first describing it and telling you about it, and then you must have their permission.

This method is based on reverse psychology and it works, even if they figure out what you're doing. You can also go over this chapter with them. They'll appreciate that you are interested in the sentimental value of their possessions.

IS SOMEONE TRYING TO FORCE YOU TO GET RID OF YOUR STUFF?

Many organizing books teach that we never access 80 percent of the things we file. So what? In truth, it may be 90 percent or even more! Far more important than accurate numbers is the satisfaction of finding something when you need it. The only time you *must* get rid of a huge amount of your stuff is if it's causing an emergency: that is, if it's endangering life or property.

If someone is pestering you to get rid of your stuff, spend some time thinking about the difference between keeping what you want and just making things look neat. Then explain it to them.

◁ Who Has Time to Toss?

We use the verb, *to cull* to mean, "to get rid of the stuff that's past its use-by date."

If you think you don't have time to cull, try this trick: Use down time. Down time is when you're stuck waiting on hold, waiting for the computer to boot, waiting for that pay increase you were promised, waiting for the printer to print, or waiting for a client to arrive. You know; time you would otherwise spend cursing.

When time's a-wasting, grab a folder and go through it. Work with just a few folders at a time, and you'll get that culling done.

◁ Here Are Those Lists

Here are four lists of what to throw out and what to keep. Remember, if you own a home, a business, property, if you have employees, or if you expect to get Social Security payments someday, be especially careful. Consult a tax or real estate attorney if you have any questions.

▷ Throw These Things Out

- Old To-Do lists (If they include tasks not done yet, transfer those tasks to new To-Do Notes)

- Business cards from people you can't remember for the life of you

- Broken items you know you'll never repair (some charities can use these)

- Pens that don't work (duh!)

- Expired warranties on items you no longer own (double duh!)

- Expenses that have been reimbursed, especially if they're more than four years old (as long as the tax man says it's OK)

- Material that has been scanned, stored elsewhere, or is no longer needed for any possible reason on earth

- Mangled papers: crumpled folders, wrinkled charts, wadded up notes, etc., if the information on them is useless

- Paid bills, except those needed for tax purposes. Keep paid bills for one year, because you never know when there will be a question. Of course you could always look at your cancelled checks by date, but unless you're a Chron ⊕, you probably won't remember what date you paid the bill, will you?

▷ **Recycle These**

- Old letterhead (cut it into quarters and use it as note paper)

- Maps (schools and libraries can use them)

- Old eyeglasses (contact your local Lions club)

- Reading material that's so old you don't care if you *ever* read it. (Again, pretend I'm going to throw it out, and decide how you feel. If you don't care, out it goes! If you *do* care, label it according to how you will use it.)

A SPECIAL NOTE ABOUT RECYCLING

Two of my clients owned a mortgage brokerage. They used recycled paper for notepads. One day I was using one of their notepads. I turned it over and there, on the back, was a client's tax return including Social Security number, address, name, and phone number—in short, all the things that would make identity theft easy.

Stay aware of privacy issues, and shred sensitive documents!

▷ **Stuff to Keep**

Keep anything you might need to prove. Many's the kingdom that was saved by documentation! This means legal, financial, and contractual paperwork, just to name a few. When in doubt, *don't* throw it out!

If you're still on the fence, pull the material and put it in a well-labeled box (under what circumstances will you want it again?) in storage. If you need it, it'll be there. You can always decide to throw it away later.

- Keep federal tax-related papers for at least three years, and state tax papers for at least four years. Check with your accountant for the law in your state, and be sure to ask about things that could come back and bite you. (Some accountants will say, "Oh, three years, that's all." Then when you get audited, they'll ask you for records that are four years old. Ask before you're audited!)

- Keep all your tax returns forever. Your Social Security payments will be based on your lifetime tax returns, and if the Social Security office gets one wrong, you will be stuck trying to prove it.

- Keep all vehicle and equipment maintenance records for as long as you have the vehicle or equipment. Having the maintenance records since the date of purchase make it easier to sell the item, because it's more attractive to the buyer when they can see how it's been serviced—and it may even affect their warranty.

- Keep frequent flyer mileage statements for the last 18 months. Why 18? If the airline changes hands, statements sent to you during the changeover may be contested by the new buyer. By showing a history, you'll have a more solid foundation.

- Keep all cancelled checks (as proof of payment for deductible items) for a minimum of seven years. Check with an accountant for the time limit in your state.

- Keep resumes that job applicants have submitted to you. Check with an employment attorney for the time limit in your state.

- Keep your critical papers (including birth certificates, health records, wills, financial paperwork and photos) in a fire-rated *and* burglar proof safe (most safes give you one rating or the other, but you can find safes with both) or off your premises in a safe deposit box. Do *not* use a safe you can push folded documents into. In case of a fire, flames can be sucked into the interior and burn the contents.

- Keep all records pertaining to your home (including home improvement receipts) forever. Keep property tax assessments for at least two years.

A GOOD WAY TO KEEP PAID BILLS

Store paid bills by the category and then the year.

Examples:
- Advertising, 2003
- Business Gifts, 2003
- Car Registration, 2003
  . . . Etc.

Ask your CPA or accountant for a Chart of Accounts (list of titles), and use them to make file folders. I use a different color for each year (for example, all the 2002 folders were aqua). This makes it very easy to pull "dead" files when the calendar clicks over.

This system satisfies all the Access Types:

🕐 Chrons can see the year

👁Visuals can see the color they associate with the year

✋Spatials can pull one year at a time

▷ Optional "Keep" List

- Awards and certificates (take them out of the frames and put them in folders in a file drawer, then recycle the frames)

- Your own resumes (for at least one year)

Chapter 18
Recapping the Magic Questions

Whenever you want to review this book, turn to this chapter. Go through these questions and you'll remember what you've learned.

If you don't have an answer for the first question, go to the second. If the second doesn't do the job, go to the third, and so on.

The more you practice these questions, the less you will need to pay outside organizing help.

1. "What is the action I need to take with this?"

2. "When does this have to be done?"

3. "What must I do before that?"

4. "How long can I put this off without creating a problem?"

5. "Who else can do this task besides me?"

6. "When will I see the person? Where will I be when I see them?"

7. "What else will I have with me when I need this?"

8. "Might I forget to do this task?"

9. "Which of these things can wait?"

10. (How to label)

    "Under what circumstances will I want to *see* this again?"

    "*Where* will I use this next time?"

    "*When* will I want to use this again?"

11. "What was the action I was going to take?"

12. "Where am I going to reach for it?"

    "Where will I be sitting when I use it?"

13. (How to file)

    "Where will I look for this?"

    "Under what word am I going to *look* for this?"

    "Where am I going to *reach* for it?"

    "*When* am I going to want it?"

14. "Who's the best person to do this task with me?"

15. "If a stranger threw this away, how would I feel about it?"

Index

A

Access 6, 16, 17, 18, 21, 22, 26, 27, 29, 31, 33, 34, 41, 96, 134, 140, 145, 178, 182, 185, 190, 193, 206, 212
Access Type 16, 17, 22, 23, 24, 25, 80, 83, 139, 144, 179, 184, 186, 218
Accessible 36, 41, 101, 192
Arrange 21, 171, 182, 229
Arrangement 47, 54, 55, 60, 61, 230

B

Basket 159
Bin 51, 52, 61, 62, 68, 84, 86, 87, 89, 90, 106 111, 112, 113, 115, 121, 124, 128, 129, 147, 152, 172, 173, 175, 186, 187, 189, 190, 191
Blockers 44, 45
Bookcase 54, 63, 118, 174, 182
Bookkeeping 38, 42
Busy 9, 152, 181, 203

C

Catchers 44, 58
Central Headquarters 77, 78, 79, 81, 184
Chron, Chronological 16, 17, 21, 22, 23, 24, 25, 42, 72, 73, 100, 101, 102, 118, 144, 145, 146, 155, 189, 214, 218
Clutter 20, 206
Collyer Brothers 208
Containers 70, 71, 73, 74, 75, 99, 119

❖ Backword

How does it feel to discover that you weren't the problem after all? What a relief to know that your furniture was disorganized, not you, and that all those people trying to change you were wrong. There's nothing that can't be fixed with a healthy respect for your habits and preferences! You just needed to get organized *your* way, didn't you? And now everything is falling into place.

Now that your system is tailored to *you*, you'll enjoy tremendous time savings and, yes, even save money. You might also find your confidence increases when you tell those Negative Nellies to leave you alone; you have things arranged as you want them, and that's that.

The more you respect your own Organizing Style, the less often you'll need to reorganize. Things won't get out of whack in the first place when they have been structured to suit you all along.

Just remember to keep your papers flowing from your In-Bin, through your Control Folders and into action, into your Holding Tanks until *you* decide to work on them, or into your inactive files, and you'll realize that circling paperwork around you is the key to staying organized.

Arrange the furniture to support your circular flow, and you're home free!

Happy Organizing!

❖ About the Author

Elizabeth (Liz) Franklin started her first business at the age of 15. A capitalist even during the hippie era, she designed and sold her own jewelry. At the ripe old age of 19, she decided that being a business secretary was the key to a glorious future. After telling her bosses how they could run their businesses better, she was heartily invited to join the ranks of the self-unemployed. Never daunted, she turned her back on free government cash to forge a new career as a business and comedy writer.

As people watched her work and observed her breathtaking sense of organization, some of them began asking her for help. As the daughter of a rocket scientist and a Virgo, Liz is a natural organizer. You can often find her in better restaurants, carefully placing the silverware at exact right angles and alphabetizing all the floral arrangements.

In 1979 Liz founded The Franklin Organization (now franklinizer.com), to root out and cure the underlying causes of disorganization. Her methods worked. The problems did not occur again. (Liz has often observed that standard time management and organizing recommendations simply do not work; a dilemma she attributes to methods that address only the symptoms, and not the causes, of disorganization.)

The better she got at organizing, the more money her clients made: As she reassured them they were not crazy and that there was a motive behind what others saw as their madness, she realized they were also becoming incredibly relaxed and prosperous.

Today Liz works with individuals and businesses, reducing their workloads, streamlining their workflow, and increasing their income. One of her clients realized a 700% increase in eight months. Another went from a personal income of $24,000 a year to $176,000 a year in one year. A third made an extra $200,000 on one business deal due to improved organization.

Liz is an internationally published author of hundreds of articles on offices, employment, delegation, management, and organization, as well as being the past publisher of "The Office Organizer," her own newsletter. In addition, Liz has made presentations to thousands of corporations, professionals and associations.

P.S. Liz Franklin is a Cross-Dominant Spatial.

❖ If You Think You'd Like to Become an Organizer . . .

. . . the best way to get a leg up is to contact NAPO, the National Association of Professional Organizers. You can log onto their Website at http://www.napo.net; they are there to help you learn about the profession. After 24 years in this business, I have received hundreds of calls from beginning organizers, and I just can't give each one the time they want to help them set up their businesses.

The big message here is this: Expect to invest a great deal of time. Becoming an organizer means devoting your energy, money, and dozens of other resources to building what is—let's face it—a business. If you behave as if you're opening a retail store or going to school to get a degree, you'll be on the right track.

As a professional organizer, get ready to be responsible for hundreds (if not thousands) of details. Just a few of them include...

- insurance for yourself (and your employees) including disability, liability, medical, dental, vision, auto and home, managing your own insurance policy purchases, your claims, and all the other paperwork required...

- licenses, fees, and registrations including a fictitious name statement, city business license, state resale license, and maybe even a national trademark for your business name...

- signing up new clients (where will you find them? how will you convince them to sign up with you?) including explaining how you do business, getting them to sign a contract or agreement, scheduling appointments and changes to appointments, dealing with sudden cancellations, shopping for furniture and supplies, and solving dozens of other problems from partners' disagreements to changes of heart...

- all forms of banking, including setting up a merchant agreement if you want to accept credit cards; invoicing, asking for, and collecting money, making bank deposits, keeping records of every transaction, developing budgets, paying bills, keeping cash records, keeping a travel diary, handling bank reconciliations...

- taxes, including planning, earning and paying them, not to mention coming up with self-employment tax deposits four times a year (you will be paying your taxes in advance) for state, and federal amounts due; also calculating, collecting and paying sales tax, city tax, and any other taxes or fees...

- if you write a book, there will be copyright fees, licensing and registration fees and processes, taxes, consulting and design fees (and dozens more) unless you go with a national publisher; either way, you will need to invest time and money in a concerted marketing effort that is easily as involved as another full-time job...

- hiring help including filing a Federal Tax I.D. number; posting ads, interviewing applicants, keeping resumes on file, meeting local, state and federal regulations, hiring and firing, paying unemployment, worker's compensation, and a host of other taxes, fees, and wages...

- your own (and your employees') financial planning, retirement planning and investments, and finding and hiring reliable people to advise you and support you in those endeavors...

- continually earning the money to pay for all of this through constant marketing, public relations, advertising, and news releases so people know you're out there, so they can find you, so they can hire you…

- designing (or having designed) and producing a logo, business cards, stationery, flyers, brochures, handouts, sales materials, etc.…

- your own office work including correspondence, filing, computer input, keeping a database of all your contacts' names and addresses, buying and managing software, office and computer equipment, warranties and service agreements…

- attending trade association meetings, networking meetings, client meetings, and a host of other meetings including possibly serving on boards, non-profits, and joining service or community groups…

- legal details including contracts, local, state, and national regulations, and more …

- constant customer service work, client relations, and everything else it takes to keep a good reputation. . .

- website writing, design, and maintenance, including e-mail

management, and gathering the
resulting information for best use. . .

- plus the usual caring for home,
family, health, pets, vehicles, etc. . .

I'm sure I've forgotten a few dozen items; if you think of them, write to me and we'll add them to the next edition of this book.

As a professional organizer, you'll be part of a growing group who'll want to see you succeed and add merit to our profession. Do a good job and make us all proud!

Good luck and happy organizing,

Liz Franklin

October 2002

❖ How to Get in Touch with Us

☎ **BY PHONE**: TOLL-FREE 877-274-0844
💻 **BY E-MAIL**: liz@franklinizer.com
🖨 **BY FAX**: 510-814-8003
🖃 **BY SNAIL MAIL**:
Liz Franklin
c/o Clara Fyer™ Books
2532 Santa Clara Ave. #406
Alameda, CA 94501, USA

MEDIA: TOLL-FREE 877-274-0844
or on line at http://www.franklinizer.com
e-mail to liz@franklinizer.com

QUANTITY DISCOUNTS:
Quantity discounts are available on bulk purchases
of this book for use as gifts, promotional items,
incentives and more. Book excerpts are available
to media for purposes of review.

REFERENCE THIS BOOK AND ISBN NUMBER:
How to Get Organized Without Resorting to Arson
by Liz Franklin
ISBN 0-9719495-6-5

❖ How to Hire Liz Franklin to Speak For Your Group

1. Go to http://www.franklinizer.com, and click on Have Liz Speak to Your Group, then fill out the form and forward it to us. If you don't have a call back within two business days, give us a call at 877-274-0844 TOLL FREE.

    OR

2. Call 877-274-0844 TOLL FREE and let us know . . .

- The name of your group

- Your contact person's name, phone number and e-mail

- The date and city of your event

- The topic you'd like Liz to speak about

- Whether you want one speech, a longer seminar, or a series of events

- How many will be in your audience

- The objective and theme of your event

. . . and anything else you'd like us to know!

❖ How to Hire Liz Franklin to Organize Your Office

1. Go to http://www.franklinizer.com, and click on Contact Us, then tell us about your situation (see below). If you don't have a call back within two business days, give us a call at 877-274-0844 TOLL FREE.

    OR

2. Call 877-274-0844 TOLL FREE and let us know the following:

    *   Your name, title, and whether you work with a partner

    *   The name of your company, if any

    *   Your phone number, fax, e-mail and what city you work in

    *   How many people need organizing

    *   The organizational problem(s) you're experiencing

    *   Your ideal organizing goal

. . . and anything else you'd like us to know!

❖ What Are People Saying About this Breakthrough Book?

"I'm astonished! I read this book and discovered $7,000 lying under lost papers. Once you follow Liz's fun but wise advice, you open the doors for money to come to you faster than you can say, 'Read this book now!'"
> — Joe Vitale, author of *Spiritual Marketing* and way too many other books to list here

"Who knew getting organized could be so much fun? Liz Franklin offers a readable, step-by-step guide that will work for you!"
> — Leda Jean Ciraolo, Owner The Written Word

"Liz Franklin throws out the tired old organizing myths and frees the hopelessly cluttered to create their own colorful path to order. It really works!"
> — Naomi Lucks, YouCanWrite.com

"Liz Franklin is really the guru for getting organized. I don't believe she has overlooked any organizational problem in her new book *How to Get Organized Without Resorting to Arson.*"
"Clever, practical, and "I wish I thought about that" is what you will be saying before you put this book down."
> — Mary Hardeman-Schulze, Publisher, Bay Area's Best Enterprises

"Liz provides essential wisdom to determine your Work Personality, Access Type, and Organizing Style. You won't believe how truly easy it is to get organized."
> — Jacqueline Kelly, Secretariat, Foundation for Intelligent Physical Agents

"Need to get organized? Adapt the process to your needs ~ instead of your needs to the process. With great wit, Liz shows you how."
> — Elizabeth A. Wright, Owner, History in Progress

❖ Quick Order Form—Four Ways to Order

☎ **BY PHONE:** TOLL-FREE 877-274-0844
🖳 **BY E-MAIL:** liz@franklinizer.com
🗐 **BY FAX:** 510-814-8003
🖃 **BY SNAIL MAIL:**

Clara Fyer™ Books
2532 Santa Clara Ave. #406
Alameda, CA 94501
USA

ORDER COPIES FOR ALL YOUR FRIENDS!

HOW TO GET ORGANIZED
WITHOUT RESORTING TO ARSON:
A Step-by-Step Guide to Clearing Your Desk
Without Panic or the Use of Open Flame

ISBN 0-9719495-6-5   272 pages with illustrations

PLEASE SEND _____ copies at $19.95

SUB-TOTAL _____

Sales tax: Please add 8.25% for books shipped to California addresses

SALES TAX _____

Shipping: U.S. $5.00 for *How to Get Organized*, .50 for each add'l book.
Int'l: $10.00 for *How to Get Organized*, 1.50 for each add'l book.

SHIPPING _____

TOTAL _____

Payment: ____Check   ____Visa   ____MasterCard
Credit Card Number: _____
Name (please print): _____
Expiration Date: _____
Signature: _____
Daytime Phone: (must have!) (_____) _____

Make check payable to Clara Fyer Books.
Thank you for your business!